CONTENTS

Introduction

PART 2: MANAGEMENT AND CONTROL

****

Introduction

Many times, I have met people who have the same common complaint, 'I dread the time when it is necessary to prepare accounts for my business. In truth, I don't understand the figures that my accountant provides and I don't understand why I have to pay tax when, according to me, I have made a loss'

This pretty much sums up both the general level of knowledge of most people when it comes to accounting, and the general principles of accounting. The annual preparation of accounts is very much like the annual visit to the dentist-both can hit you in the pocket.

It is true to say that most people who run businesses would rather get on with the process and leave the accounting to others. However, a knowledge of accounting, even a basic knowledge can help and assist with the daily running of a business. A knowledge of accounting will also help you to converse with your accountant and to understand how you can change things to make your business more profitable. Quite often accountants will accept what you give them and use the information on which to base their final figures, whereas with a working knowledge of accounting you can help shape your own business so it is more profitable.

Reading this book won't turn you into a fully qualified accountant That is a rather more drawn-out process. It should however, turn you into a better manager. The main purpose of accounting, as we will see, is to:

- Provide a system that will record income and expenditure relating to the day-to-day activities of your particular business. This regular recording of data is absolutely necessary for the annual completion of accounts and tax returns and also helps potential funders and future business partners assess the business.

- Accounting provides a tool for analysing your business and assessing overall performance. With a little knowledge you can make more informed decisions about your business and how to improve performance.

In this book, from the start we cover the very basics of accounting and bookkeeping and also the preparation of key financial statements. We also cover taxation and VAT. Each area is illustrated.

Finally, we then cover management accounting, which is about the provision of information to make decisions. This section is more suited to larger businesses, typically limited companies although the information will still be useful for anyone engaged in business.

I will outline how to use ratio analysis techniques to spot trends and key figures in business, which is more about management accounting. Overall, you should find this book informative and rewarding and use the information gleaned to help you better manage your business or to develop your knowledge for future management.

It is important to note that this book does not cover Public Liability companies (PLC's) as this is a totally different and somewhat more complex area of accounting. The information contained within is appropriate to sole traders, partners and limited companies.

****

Chapter 1

Fundamentals of Accounting

In chapter 1 we will look at the following:
- A Definition of accounting and different areas of accounting.
- Different business entities
- Basic accounting terms

This will serve as a backdrop to the following chapters, which go into detail about the practice of bookkeeping and production of accounts.

A definition of accounting

Technically speaking, "Bookkeeping" means the ongoing **recording** of business transactions in Books of Account. "Accounting" means **taking financial information** from the books of account and using it to explain and understand the financial position of the business.

Accounts are a summary of a businesses financial activities for a period of time, commonly 12 months. Accounts can also be referred to as financial statements. A business will need accounts to see how the business is doing, to raise money for the business (bank managers will always want to see accounts), to raise money for the owners, i.e. for loans and mortgages, for insurance claims, for making tax returns, for partners in a partnership to see what is their share, for businesses which are a company for filing with

Companies House and, finally, when it comes to sell the business then the purchaser will want to see past and current accounts. Accounting information you have prepared will show:

- Whether the business is making a profit or a loss
- What is the value of a business
- What is the cash situation
- Who owes what to a business
- Overall, how the business is performing

Therefore, the main purpose of accounting is the clear provision of information to those who wish to make decisions, including you as the owner.

The Accounting Cycle

All of the transactions, and statements produced during the day-to-day activities of a business, culminating in the final accounts, follow a pre-determined seven-stage cycle as set out below, starting with the daily activity of the business (transactions). Different companies have their own internal accounting cycles and it is stressed that the stages set out below, which are universal, are for the learning purposes of this book.

- *Stage 1.* Business transactions – the active trading of the business, which is the start of the whole cycle and which generates money.

- *Stage 2.* Maintenance of Day books – recording those transactions and starting to create a picture of the business activities.
- *Stage 3.* Development of the Double entry system of accounts and Ledgers (maintenance of separate books for each area of trading)
- *Stage 4.* Formulation of the Trial Balance – balancing of the books on a periodic basis
- *Stage 5*. Period end adjustments – any adjustments that need to be made to books as time goes on
- *Stage 6.* Production of financial statements (Accounts)
- *Stage 7*. Period Close – end of financial year

Accordingly, this book will follow each stage, setting out practical examples. The stages are the same, notwithstanding the type of business you run, or what structure you choose to adopt. Below is an outline of the main business structures

Types of business entities
Businesses can be Sole Traders, Partnerships, a Limited Company or a Limited Liability partnership. As stated this book doesn't deal with PLC's. What binds all business is the need to keep books of account and present final accounts to HMRC.

Sole Trader
This is a self-employed individual who is personally financially responsible if things go wrong, for example if the business cannot

pay its debts and taxes. If problems occur, the individuals home and assets may be at risk.

A Partnership

This is more than one self-employed person working together to make a profit and sharing everything on an agreed split. Each partner is personally responsible for all debts run up by the partnership as a whole except for tax debts (individuals are responsible for their own tax debts).

A Limited Company

This is a separate legal structure where the liability of owners of the business is limited to the amount of their shares. Any legal action has to be against the company not the shareholders and the shareholders personal assets are safe. (See chapter 6)

A Limited Liability Partnership

This has many of the features of a normal partnership-but it is like a limited company in that members of the LLP cannot usually lose more than they invest.

**

The role of Accountants

Within the context of the business world, accountants have several roles as set out below. For the majority of readers of this book, financial accountants will have the most relevance. However, it is worth knowing about the wider activities of the accounting world.

Financial Accounting

Financial accounting, or financial reporting, is the process of producing information for external use usually in the form of financial statements. Financial Statements reflect a businesses past performance and current position based on a set of standards and guidelines known as GAAP (Generally Accepted Accounting Principles). GAAP refers to the standard framework of guidelines for financial accounting used in any given jurisdiction. This generally includes accounting standards (e.g. International Financial Reporting Standards), accounting conventions, and rules and regulations that accountants must follow in the preparation of the financial statements.

Management Accounting

Management accounting produces information primarily for internal use by the company's management. In Part 2 chapters 8 and 9 we cover management accounting in more detail. The information produced is generally more detailed than that produced for external use to enable effective organizational control and the fulfillment of the strategic aims and objectives of the business. Information may be in the form of budgets and forecasts, enabling an enterprise to plan effectively for its future or may include an assessment based on its past performance and results. The form and content of any report produced in the process is purely upon management's discretion. Cost accounting is a branch of management accounting and involves the application of various techniques to monitor and control costs. Its application is more suited to manufacturing concerns.

Governmental Accounting,

Governmental accounting, also known as public accounting or federal accounting, refers to the type of accounting information system used in the public sector. This is a slight deviation from the financial accounting system used in the private sector. The need to have a separate accounting system for the public sector arises because of the different aims and objectives of the state owned and privately owned institutions. Governmental accounting ensures the financial position and performance of the public sector institutions are set in a budgetary context since financial constraints are often a major concern of most governments. Separate rules are followed in many jurisdictions to account for the transactions and events of public entities.

Tax Accounting

Tax accounting refers to accounting for tax related matters. It is governed by the tax rules prescribed by the tax laws of a jurisdiction. Often these rules are different from the rules that govern the preparation of financial statements for public use (i.e. GAAP). Tax accountants therefore adjust the financial statements prepared under financial accounting principles to account for the differences with rules prescribed by the tax laws.

18

Information is then used by tax professionals to estimate the tax liability of a company and for tax planning purposes.

Forensic Accounting

Forensic accounting is the use of accounting, auditing and investigative techniques in cases of litigation or disputes. Forensic accountants act as expert witnesses in courts of law in civil and criminal disputes that require an assessment of the financial effects of a loss or the detection of a financial fraud. Common litigations where forensic accountants are hired include insurance claims, personal injury claims, suspected fraud and claims of professional negligence in a financial matter (e.g. business valuation).

Project Accounting

Project accounting refers to the use of accounting systems to track the financial progress of a project through frequent financial reports. Project accounting is a vital component of project management. It is a specialized branch of management accounting with a prime focus on ensuring the financial success of company projects such as the launch of a new product. Project accounting can be a source of competitive advantage for project-oriented businesses such as construction firms.

Social Accounting

Social accounting, also known as Corporate Social Responsibility Reporting and Sustainability Accounting, refers to the process of reporting implications of an organization's activities on its ecological and social environment. Social Accounting is primarily reported in the form of Environmental Reports accompanying the annual reports of companies. Social Accounting is still in the early stages of development and is considered to be a response to the growing environmental consciousness amongst the public at large.

**

Basic accounting terms

Many of these terms are repeated in the glossary at the back of this book. and will be found as we travel through the various chapters However, it is worthwhile getting to know them at the outset.

- **Accounting period:** The time period for which financial information is being tracked. Most businesses track their financial results on a monthly basis, so each accounting period equals one month. Some businesses choose to do financial reports on a quarterly or annual basis. Businesses that track their financial activities monthly usually also create quarterly and annual reports.

- **Accounts payable:** The account used to track all outstanding bills from vendors, contractors, consultants, and any other companies or individuals from whom the company buys goods or services.

- **Accounts receivable:** The account used to track all customer sales that are made by store credit. *Store credit* refers not to credit card sales but rather to sales in which the customer is given credit directly by the store and the store needs to collect payment from the customer at a later date.

- **Accruals:** The accruals (or matching) concept is fundamental to the preparation of accounts. The concept simply means that income and expenditure is accounted for when a transaction occurs, not when cash is paid.

- **Assets:** All the things a company owns in order to successfully run its business, such as cash, buildings, land, tools, equipment, vehicles, and furniture. Assets are often divided into non-current assets and current assets. Non-current assets are assets which tend to be a more long-term feature of the business, such as business premises or office furnoture. Current assets are short term in nature and are typically turned into cash within an accounting year. Examples would be stock held in a business or cash in the bank.

- **Balance sheet:** The financial statement that presents a snapshot of the company's financial position as of a particular date in time. It's called a balance sheet because the things owned by the company (*assets*) must equal the claims against those assets (*liabilities* and *equity*).

- **Capital.** What makes up capital depends on the type of business. In sole trader or partnership situations, capital is the money personally invested in a business. In a limited company, capital consists of the value of shares bought by shareholders of a company.

- **Costs of goods sold:** All money spent to purchase or make the products or services a company plans to sell to its customers.

- **Depreciation:** An accounting method used to track the aging and use of assets. For example, if you own a car, you know that each year you use the car it's value is reduced (unless you own one of those classic cars that goes up in value). Every major asset a business owns ages and eventually needs replacement, including buildings, factories, equipment, and other key assets.

- **Equity:** All the money invested in the company by its owners. In a small business owned by one person or a group of people, the owner's equity is shown in a Capital account. In a larger business that is incorporated, owner's equity is shown in shares of stock. Another key Equity account is *Retained Earnings,* which tracks all company profits that have been reinvested in the company rather than paid out to the company's owners. Small businesses track money paid out to owners in a Drawing account, whereas incorporated businesses dole out money to owners by paying dividends.

- **Expenditure:** This is expenses incurred by the business. It must be expenditure for the business alone to be classified as expenditure.

- **General Ledger:** Where all the company's accounts are summarized. The General Ledger is the granddaddy of the bookkeeping system.

- **Income:** Income generally means the amounts generated by selling products or services to customers, but it also includes items such as bank interest, or income from investments which would be termed 'other income'.

- **Income statement:** The financial statement that presents a summary of the company's financial activity over a certain period of time, such as a month, quarter, or year. The statement starts with Revenue earned, subtracts the Costs of Goods Sold and the Expenses, and ends with the bottom line — Net Profit or Loss.

- **Interest:** The money a company needs to pay if it borrows money from a bank or other company. For example, when you buy a car using a car loan, you must pay not only the amount you borrowed but also interest, based on a percent of the amount you borrowed.

- **Inventory:** The account that tracks all products that will be sold to customers.

- **Journals:** Where bookkeepers keep records (in chronological order) of daily company transactions. Each of the most active accounts—including cash, Accounts Payable, and Accounts Receivable—has its own journal.

- **Liabilities:** All the debts the company owes, such as bonds, loans, and unpaid bills. A liability arises from a past business transaction. For example, a purchase of goods on credit. If you have 30 days credit then there is an obligation (liability) to pay at some point after the transaction occurs. Like assets, liabilities are classified as current and non-current. Current liabilities are normally repayable within one year, with non-current liabilities payable after more than one year. Typical examples of current liabilities are amounts owed to suppliers, tax authorities and bank repayments. Examples of non-current liabilities are bank loans or mortgages.

- **Payroll:** The way a company pays its employees. Managing payroll is a key function of the bookkeeper and involves reporting many aspects of payroll to the government, including taxes to be paid on behalf of the employee, unemployment taxes, and workman's compensation.

- **Revenue:** All money collected in the process of selling the company's goods and services. Some companies also collect revenue through other means, such as selling assets the business no longer needs or earning interest by offering short-term loans to employees or other businesses.

- **Trial balance:** How you test to be sure the books are in balance before pulling together information for the financial reports and closing the books for the accounting period.

The above are the main concepts that you will encounter in day-to-day accounting. In the next section, we will start at the very beginning and look at the main principles of bookkeeping, which will start the process of recording transactions and build up to the final accounts.

****

Chapter 2

Basic Bookkeeping

Stages 1 and 2 of the accounting cycle-generating money-business transactions and recording those transactions.

In chapter 2, we look closely at the basic elements of bookkeeping, which forms one of the day-to-day activities of running a business, whether sole trader, limited company or partnership. We look at what information should be kept, the advantages of a good bookkeeping system, the recording of information, and also give examples of how to record transactions.

Business activities of a company or enterprise

In chapter 1, we outlined the seven stages of the accounting cycle, stage one of which is the day to day activities of the company, or enterprise. Your business activities, in common with all businesses, will consist of selling goods and/or services. At the same time you will have to spend money on behalf of the business, on the purchase or rent of premises, wages or salaries, raw materials, equipment, stationery etc. etc. in order to conduct business.

The main point is that every business transaction generates a financial transaction, all of which must be recorded in books of account on an ongoing basis. This is stage 2 of the cycle.

27

It is a fundamental management requirement that this be done on a regular basis, at a minimum once a week. Leave it much longer, and sooner or later an iron law of accounting will come into operation. You will have mislaid a financial record or simply forgotten to request one or issue one. When you do get around to up-dating the books, they won't balance. Unless you can discover the error before the end of the financial year your accountant, if you have one, will be faced with the task of reconciling "incomplete records", which he or she will enjoy because of the professional challenge but which costs you more money for more of his/her time.

What information must be kept?

As a minimum you must keep records of the following:

i) All the invoices raised (or rendered) on behalf of the business, An invoice is a legal document and it constitutes a formal demand for money. It must provide enough information to identify the business which sent it, who it was sent to, what it is for and whether VAT is payable. These invoices should be numbered sequentially. See further on for an example invoice.

ii) All Purchase invoices received, and listed i.e. those demands made on your business for the payment of money.

iv) Wages and salaries paid, and to whom; Income tax and NI contributions paid over to the Tax authorities. Also, pension contributions.

28

v) All chequebook stubs, paying-in slips/books, counterfoils of petty cash vouchers, business bank account statements. Without these you cannot compile your books of account.

vi) A full record of VAT, whether paid by or paid to the business.

These records will be kept, initially, in main, or prime, books of account, as we will see.

The advantages of a good bookkeeping system for your business
Following on from this, you need a bookkeeping system that mirrors your day-to-day activity.

The fundamental purpose of a bookkeeping system is :

a) To provide accurate information sufficient to assess whether you are managing the business at a profit or a loss, or whether the business is solvent i.e. is there enough cash available in the business to pay all the outstanding liabilities on demand? The right information of the right kind at the right time is a vital management tool. Good management means making informed decisions of the right kind at the right time based on information that is true and therefore trustworthy.

b) To provide the information required for correct assessments of VAT and Income Tax, so as to avoid financial penalties (and possibly a suspect reputation) for incorrect and/or late payments.

HM Revenue and Customs keeps records for seven years. Your accountant will need the best information in order to minimise your tax liabilities, unless of course you decide to submit a statement of income to your Inspector of Taxes without recourse to an accountant. In any event the Inspector will require a calculation of your Income from the business in the form of an Income and Expenditure Account for each trading year.

c) To monitor the behaviour of the business over time by reference to financial summaries "at a glance". You don't need to remember for example how many bricks were sold in your building materials business in this financial year compared with last year. The comparison that matters is the financial one with reference to the value of those transactions.

How to record the information you need
There are, basically, three methods of bookkeeping, outlined below. These are the:

- **Proprietary system** usually used by a small trader or sole trader;
- **The single entry system** (also known as the analysed cash book system) which is most commonly used and which entails keeping books of account, the information from which is transferred to;
- **The Double entry system** to build up books of account. Which one to choose will depend largely on the type and

size of business you have established. Take advice from a business adviser or accountant if you are unsure as to which is the best one for your needs.

Most businesses nowadays will use computing software for speed and accuracy, which will encompass all of the above systems.

a) Proprietary systems.

These are best suited for sole traders in cash transaction types of business, e.g. jobbing builders, market traders or some small shopkeepers. This type of business requires daily record keeping, often including till-rolls for the cash till and offers a simple method of control over finances. In reality, most small business people would use a spreadsheet or software, as mentioned above, but this book is all about learning accounting basics! If you are using a manual system a number of pre-printed stationery books are available at business bookshops. Select one that allows you enough space to record all that needs recording. Worked examples are set out at the beginning of each book to show you how to keep cash records and the bank position, which can be calculated by following the instructions included. Cash businesses are more vulnerable than other types for the following reasons: -

i) It is far easier to lose or misplace paperwork. Therefore it is easier to lose control and lose money. It is more difficult to plan for the future.

ii) It is far more difficult to separate the cash that belongs in the business from the cash belonging to the proprietor.

iii) HMRC pays far closer attention to cash businesses because of the greater scope for "creative accounting" and tax evasion.

b) The Cash Book System (single entry).

This is perhaps the most common method used by small businesses selling mostly on credit, with perhaps some cash sales. It relies on the Single Entry system of bookkeeping, where each entry is, as the name implies, made once only, and all entries are made in one (of a number) of books. (see further on for examples).

The cashbook is the "bible" of the business where business transactions are initially recorded from source documents such as invoices, receipts, bank transfers etc. It allows "at a glance" analysis because it is arranged on a columnar basis, showing how much has been received into the business, when and from where, how much of each receipt is attributable to VAT and therefore how much is the net amount belonging to the business. At some point the entries from the accounts books will find their way onto ledgers, through the double entry system of accounting.

Although most people or organisations now use software systems, for the purposes of learning, before you can understand accounting software you need to understand the accounting process, which is why we are laying out a manual system of bookkeeping. There will usually be six account books as follows:

- The Sales Book-this will record credit sales (or sales on credit)

- The corresponding purchases book which will record purchases on credit
- The Cash Book, or cash receipts book, which records cash received from customers and any other sources.
- The Cheque payments book which records payments made by cheque or debits from the bank account belonging to the business
- The petty cash book which, as its name suggests will record all minor cash expenses going out of the business
- Finally, a general book which records any transactions not made by the other books.

Example 1-The sales account book

Peters Building Supplies Ltd						
Sales account Book						
Date	Ref	Total	sales @ 20%	10%	VAT	
14/11/17	Inv 32	£750	600		£150	
19/11/2017	Inv 33	£300	£240		£60	
22/11/17	Inv 34	£1500	£1200		£300	
Total		£2550	£2040		£510	

As mentioned, the Sales account book records sales made on credit. The source documents are the sales invoices, as per the above example. Most business will make sales on credit, usually setting their terms at 28 days, or whatever they have agreed with the business involved. You will see that the VAT rate is set at 20% although an extra column is set at 10% for a different VAT rate if applicable. By maintaining your day books this way you are keeping a running total of VAT charged.

Example 2-The Purchases Account Book

Peters Building Supplies Ltd					
Purchases account Book					
Date	Ref	Total	sales @ 20%	10%	VAT
14/11/17	16	£400	320		£80
16/11/17	17	£550	430		110
22/11/17	18	£760	608		152
Total		£1710	£1358		£342

The Purchases Account Book records purchases made on credit. The source documents are the suppliers invoices. You will see that the VAT rate is set at 20% although an extra column is set at 10% for a different VAT rate if applicable. The Purchase account Book is similar to the Sales account Book however the reference column will show the invoice number of the suppliers invoice

Example 3-Cash Receipt Book

Peters Building Supplies Ltd								
Cash Receipts Book								
Date	Detail	Ref	Total	20%	10%	MISC	VAT	Paid In

The Cash Receipts Book, as the name suggest, records all cash received by a business, which is usually paid into a bank account.

Sources of cash into a business would usually be from cash sales, cash received from customers allowed credit. There will also be miscellaneous cash. Cash sales are usually made to customers who do not have credit, such as the general public.. In the layout of a typical Cash Sales Book above. you will see columns as follows:

- Date,
- Detail of sale,
- The reference number assigned to it
- Total amount,
- VAT at two rates
- A Miscellaneous column which details odd sums
- VAT amount
- The amount paid into the bank.

Although two entries have been made, during the course of the business many more entries will be made with the running totals adjusting accordingly.

Example 4-Cheque/bank transfer Payment Books

(Overleaf)

Peters Building Supplies Ltd

Cheque payments

Date Misc	Detail	Chq ref	Total	Creditors	Utilities	Wages	Phone	VAT
17/10	M Ltd	621326	400	400				
Total			400	400				

Different businesses will have different ways of laying out cheque payment books. The payment may also be a bank transfer so the cheque ref could also be a transfer ref. The above is pretty standard and the book is laid out as follows:

- Date
- Detail-to whom cheque payment made
- The cheque number which helps you to track payments
- The total
- A Creditors column to show that the payment was made to a trade creditor
- Whether the payment was for a utility such as electricity or gas
- Wages
- Phone
- Any VAT element
- A Miscellaneous column for any miscellaneous payment

Again, I have indicated one payment but in reality there would be many with running totals.

Example 5-Petty Cash Book

Peters Building Supplies Ltd								
Petty cash book								
Date			Paid out	Item	Total	Teas	Office	Other
17/10	Balance	75	17/10	Sugar	2.50	2.50		
18/10	Cheque	£30	18/10	cleaner	£15		£15	
Total		£105			£17.50	£17.50		

Petty Cash Books run on what is known as the imprest system. This basically means that a certain petty cash balance is maintained and topped up at regular intervals. The second column shows a balance of £75 topped up by a cheque of £30. The columns show amount spent, on what and the overall totals spent. Of course businesses can keep what form of petty cash record they want as long as a clear record is maintained.

Example 6- The General Day Book or Journal

The general day book is the final day book and it records transactions that are not recorded elsewhere. The journal is typically used to enter any corrections to minor errors made in the other day books.

Peters building supplies Ltd			
Journal			
Date	Account	Debit	Credit
17/10/2017	Write off bad debt	£2,000	
	Foreman Ltd		£2,000

This journal simply shows the date and columns for the narrative explaining what the entry is related to plus debit and credit. In this case, we have a bad debt that will not be paid. This can't be recorded in any other day book so goes in the general journal.

Invoices

It is important that you are consistent with the types of invoice that you use and to make sure that they are sequentially numbered when they are entered onto the appropriate account book

See example invoice overleaf.

Example Invoice

<table>
<tr><td colspan="2" align="center">**INVOICE**</td></tr>
<tr><td>From: Peters Building Supplies Ltd</td><td>Invoice number 32</td></tr>
<tr><td>16 Merrygate</td><td></td></tr>
<tr><td>Merrytown</td><td></td></tr>
<tr><td>Anywhere</td><td></td></tr>
<tr><td>To: David James Building- 32 Anywhere</td><td></td></tr>
<tr><td>Date: 14/11/2019</td><td></td></tr>
<tr><td>VAT Registration number 12345678</td><td></td></tr>
<tr><td>Goods</td><td>£600</td></tr>
<tr><td>VAT</td><td>£150</td></tr>
<tr><td>**Total:**</td><td>**£750**</td></tr>
<tr><td>With Thanks</td><td></td></tr>
<tr><td>Payable within 28 days</td><td></td></tr>
</table>

Of course, businesses can use any design they wish as long as you have all of the important information, such as VAT number, date, amount, from whom and to whom.

VAT

It is very important indeed that clear and accurate records are kept of VAT transactions, such as sales and receipts. In addition, your invoices, if you are VAT registered, should always indicate your VAT number. The examples above enable you to record VAT as a running total. We cover VAT in chapter 5.

The Double Entry System

This method of recording accounts builds on the maintenance of account books detailed above and, as we shall see in the next chapter, relies on ledgers, or **separate books of account** for each type of transaction. All entries in the account books are recorded in sub-accounts called 'ledgers' in order to differentiate financial information'.

Computerised Accounting Systems

Computerised accounting, using accounting software involves making use of computers and software to record, store and analyse financial data. As explained, although most businesses now use software to provide an accounting system, it is essential to understand the main principles underlying accounting for business before using accounting packages. This is what this book is about.

A computerized accounting system brings with it many advantages that are unavailable to manual accounting systems. Quick books, heavily advertised on TV is one such system but there are many others, such as Sage.

The numerous advantages of using computerized accounting software are:

Automation: Since all the calculations are handled by the software, computerized accounting eliminates many of the mundane and time-consuming processes associated with manual accounting. For example, once issued, invoices are processed automatically making accounting less time-consuming.

Accuracy: This accounting system is designed to be accurate to the tiniest detail. Once the data is entered into the system, all the calculations, including additions and subtractions, are done automatically by software.

Data Access: Using accounting software, it becomes much easier for different individuals to access accounting data outside of the office, securely.

Reliability: Because the calculations are so accurate, the financial statements prepared by computers are highly reliable.

Scalability: When your company grows, the amount of accounting necessary not only increases but becomes more complex. With computerized accounting, everything is kept straightforward because sifting through data using software is easier than sifting through a pile of papers.

Speed: Using accounting software, the entire process of preparing accounts becomes faster. Furthermore, statements and reports can be generated instantly at the click of a button. Managers do not have to wait for hours, even days, to lay their hands on an important report.

Security: The latest data can be saved and stored in offsite locations so it is safe from natural and man-made disasters like fires, floods, arson and terrorist attacks. In case of a disasters, the system can be quickly restored on other computers.

Cost-effective: Since using computerized accounting is more efficient than paper-based accounting, and work will be done faster and time will be saved.

Visuals: Viewing your accounts using a computer allows you to take advantage of the option to view your data in different formats. You can view data in tables and using different types of charts.

*

Summary of main points from Chapter 2.

- Your business activities, in common with all businesses, will consist of selling goods and/or services. At the same time you will have to spend money on behalf of the business, on the purchase or rent of premises, wages or salaries, raw materials, equipment, stationery etc. etc. in order to conduct business.

- The main point is that every business transaction generates a financial transaction, all of which must be recorded in books of account on an ongoing basis. .

- Following on from this, you need a bookkeeping system that mirrors your day-to-day activity.

- The method of bookkeeping used will depend on the type of business involved. The most common bookkeeping system used is the single entry (analysed) system-which in turn builds up information for recording onto a double entry (Ledger) system.

****

Chapter 3

Formulating Accounts-The Double Entry System

Stages 3 and 4 of the accounting cycle-maintaining ledgers and creating sub-accounts.

In chapter 3, we will look at the formulation of basic accounts for your business, starting by looking at the practice of using the Double Entry bookkeeping system and creating accounts from this system. The Double Entry system builds on the single entry system shown in the previous chapter to provide more detailed information.

As we have seen in chapter 2, "Bookkeeping" means the recording of business transactions in Books of Account. However, "Accounting" means taking financial information from those books of account and using it to explain and understand the financial position of the business.

This chapter explores more fully the relationship between the two functions, by introducing the Double Entry system of bookkeeping and the creation of accounts which are maintained separately from the Account Books but which draw their information from those Books.

Double entry bookkeeping - What is double entry bookkeeping?

Double entry bookkeeping is a system of accounting in which every transaction has a corresponding positive and negative entry (debits and credits) The double entry system of bookkeeping is based on the fact that every transaction has two parts and that this will therefore affect two ledger accounts. Every transaction involves a debit entry in one account and a credit entry in another account. This means that every transaction must be recorded in two accounts; one account will be debited because it receives value and the other account will be credited because it has given value.

To make it easier to remember, the main rule is to: "**debit the receiver and credit the giver**".

Origins of double entry bookkeeping

The double entry system can largely be credited with the development of modern accounting. It defined the methods for accurate record keeping across any industry. Historical records indicate that the double entry bookkeeping system was first seen used by merchants as early as the Middle Ages. This was a vast improvement from the abacus and early single-entry systems used from the age of Antiquity. As double entry bookkeeping became more widely used, it extended to include detailed descriptions of products and services, income, expenses, loans, bad debt, etc.'.

In the ledger

Whether hand written or computerised, the ledger contains accounts of each asset and liability of the business and of the capital (amount invested) of the owner, and a separate account is kept for every item involved in business dealings. The double entry system requires two entries for each transaction: a debit and a credit. Any purchases, such as raw materials or assets, as well as any payments from customers, must all be recorded in two places in the ledger under this system.

For example: Peter's business purchases £1,500 of raw materials from a supplier, which he will use to develop products that he will then sell to his customers. When he records this under the double entry system, he would debit his inventory account as an asset, and credit his cash account.

David runs a carpentry business and invoices a customer (Peter) a dining table for £800. This transaction would be recorded as:

- A debit of £800 in his accounts receivable.
- A credit of £800 to his revenue account.

Another, simpler example is if someone transacts a purchase of a drink from a local store, he pays cash to the shopkeeper and in return, he gets a bottle of drink. This simple transaction has two effects from the perspective of both, the buyer as well as the seller. The buyer's cash balance would decrease by the amount of the cost of purchase while on the other hand he will acquire a bottle of drink. Conversely, the seller will be one drink short though his cash balance would increase by the price of the drink.

More detailed accounts would also include a double entry approach to manage inventory and cost of goods sold.

For Every Transaction: The Value of Debits must = The Value of Credits. The accounting equation must balance the totals found in the debit and in the credit accounts:

Debits are on the left and increase a debit account and reduce a credit account. Credits are on the right and increase a credit account and decrease a debit account.

Which side should your entry be on?

Every account has two "sides", a right side and a left side. A debit refers to an entry on the left side of an account, and a credit refers to an entry on the right side of an account. Double entry bookkeeping requires that for every transaction, there is an entry to the left side of one (or more) account, and a corresponding entry to the right side of another account(s).

- Expenses are always debits
- Revenues are always credits
- Debit the cash account when cash is received
- Credit the cash account when cash is paid out

Following on from the above, the Double Entry method of recording accounts builds on the maintenance of account books and relies on **ledgers,** or **separate books of account** for each type of transaction. Basically, all entries in the account books are recorded in 'ledgers'. Far greater detail and control is possible using this system. Each ledger account is a history of money values of a particular aspect of a business.

There are three ledgers-the sales ledger, the purchases ledger and the nominal (general) ledger. The sales and purchases ledgers holds details of transactions relating to sales and purchases grouped by customer and supplier. These are known as the **Personal Ledger**.

The Nominal Ledger contains impersonal accounts and is the ledger most often used by accountants to draw up trial balances.

As sated above, for every type of transaction, from buying new machinery to paying a supplier, there will be a separate account (Ledger) and each account will look roughly as follows;

Peters Building Supplies Ltd

DR		NAME OF ACCOUNT (Salaries)		CR	
year		£	Year		£
Date/Month	Details	Amount	Date/Month	Details	Amount
DR	**NAME OF ACCOUNT (Rent and Building Costs)**				**CR**
year		£	Year		£
Date/Month	Details	Amount	Date/Month	Details	Amount

DR		NAME OF ACCOUNT (Machinery and IT)		CR	
year		£	Year		£
Date/Month	Details	Amount	Date/Month	Details	Amount

DR **NAME OF ACCOUNT (Building supplies)**			CR		
year		£	Year		£
Date/Month	Details	Amount	Date/Month	Details	Amount

DR **NAME OF ACCOUNT (Any)**		CR			
year		£	Year		£
Date/Month	Details	Amount	Date/Month	Details	Amount

DR **NAME OF ACCOUNT (Any)**				CR	
year		£	Year		£
Date/Month	Details	Amount	Date/Month	Details	Amount

DR **NAME OF ACCOUNT Any)**			CR		
year		£	Year		£
Date/Month	Details	Amount	Date/Month	Details	Amount

DR **NAME OF ACCOUNT (Any)**		CR			
year		£	Year		£
Date/Month	Details	Amount	Date/Month	Details	Amount

And so on. The number of accounts will depend on the business. Each heading is as follows:

- **Name of account** - the area that the transaction covers. There will be an account for cash, an account for every type of expense (insurance, rent and so on), an account for each type of asset (things like equipment, premises and machinery), as well as an account for each customer we sell to and each supplier we buy from (the personal accounts).

- **Date/month** - the time when the transaction is undertaken

- **Details** - the other account that is affected by the double entry transactions. Having the details here will help us to remember that there must always be two entries for each transaction.

- **Amount** - the total monetary amount of the transaction.

For each different type of account there will be different rules governing which side of the account it is entered into. This rule will depend upon whether the amount in the account is increasing or decreasing, and also whether the account is an asset, liability or a capital account. The account will always be split into two sides. Further, in addition to sub-accounts it is important to note that three further types of accounts need to be maintained:

- Asset accounts
- Liability accounts
- Capital accounts

Assets

Assets are any resources that are to be used in the business. Examples would include machinery, premises, stocks of goods and cash.

Liabilities

Liabilities refer to any borrowings undertaken by the firm to a third party, for example amounts owed to suppliers, bank overdrafts, loans, etc.

Capital

Capital refers to the value of the resources put into the firm by the owner(s). Some items can be classified as both an asset and capital. For example, cash introduced into the firm by the owner would be classed as capital. However, this cash would also be classed as an asset. This is simply the result of classifying items from two points of view. Try not to see assets as being good and liabilities as being bad. The term liability simply refers to the source of the finance, and makes no judgement on whether it is good or bad for the firm. The rules for entering these types of transactions in the double-entry accounts are as follows:

See overleaf.

ANY ASSET ACCOUNT	
INCREASES ARE ENTERED ON THIS SIDE	REDUCTIONS ARE ENTERED ON THIS SIDE

ANY LIABILITY ACCOUNT	
REDUCTIONS ARE ENTERED ON THIS SIDE	INCREASES ARE ENTERED ON THIS SIDE

ANY CAPITAL ACCOUNT	
REDUCTIONS ARE ENTERED ON THIS SIDE	INCREASES ARE ENTERED ON THIS SIDE

Accounting for purchases and sales

As we have seen. we need to keep accounts for stock being purchased and stock being sold. In fact, we actually keep four accounts for movements in stock and these are as follows:

Increases in stock

- Purchases account - stocks of goods bought by the firm for resale

- Returns inwards account - stocks previously sold that is returned by the customer due to the goods being unsuitable (e.g. they are damaged, the wrong type of goods, etc.)

Decreases in stock

- Sales account - stocks of goods sold to customers
- Returns outwards account - stocks previously purchased by the firm which is returned to the original supplier

The normal double entry rules apply to all these stock accounts. Stock is an asset therefore, increases in stocks will always be debited to the relevant account and decreases will always be credited.

Accounting for expenses and revenues

All firms will have expenses to pay as part of normal business activity. This will occur on a frequent basis. Each separate expense will have its own account. Expenses do not fall into the classification of 'asset', 'liability' or 'capital', but we can still work out the rules for making entries in the expense accounts.

Any expense will require either cash or a cheque payment (or BACS). Therefore, this will require a credit entry in either the cash or the bank account. As a result, the debit entry must be in the expense.

Accounting for drawings

Earlier in this section we saw that anything injected into the business for use in the business by the owner is known as capital. However, it is perfectly possible for the owner to withdraw resources (money or stock for example) from the business. This would be represented by a decrease in capital. These reductions are known as 'drawings'.

These 'drawings' are kept in a separate drawings account - which is another form of capital account and follows the same double entry rules.

DEBTORS

This is the term used to describe those who owe money to the business. Debtors represent an asset of a business and therefore appear only in the Balance Sheet.

You would have adopted one of two methods to record and monitor the situation with debtors:

a) You may have "lumped" them all together in one aggregate Debtors Account; or

b) Separated them out into named Debtor accounts, so as to more closely monitor the comparative progress of each and to maintain closer control of the most important. At the end of the year, in order to compile a summary of debtors, you will need to collate the final balances on each separate account to arrive at an aggregate Debtors account.

BAD AND DOUBTFUL DEBTS

At the end of the year there will almost certainly be customers who have not paid what they owe when the Final Accounts are compiled. Some of those debts will be paid during the course of the following financial year. But you may have doubts as to whether they will all be paid in full, or when.

If neither the debt nor the goods can be recovered then the remaining option is to cut your losses and write-off the debt from the books. In this case the sum becomes a bad Debt and must be treated in the appropriate way. First the bad debt must be transferred from the Debtors account, since it is no longer an asset, to a Bad Debt account. Since Bad debts will be shown as DR or Debit entries, it follows that the entries to reduce the Debtors account will be CR or Credit entries, in accordance with the double entry rules.

Doubtful Debts are different. They are by implication those you are not sure about. Again the procedure is to create a special account by transferring doubtful debts to a "Doubtful Debt Provision Account". The balance on this account will be shown separately as set-off (or subtracted from) the Debtors account in the Balance Sheet, which will then indicate the net amount believed to be collectable.

Any provision for doubtful debts will also appear as an item in the Profit and Loss account as a "Doubtful Debt Provision", as an Expense, because it represents an anticipated though not yet proven Expense that will be borne by the business. Again, like the Bad Debt account, a Doubtful Debt Provision account will show DR or Debit entries, according to the double entry rules.

Depreciation of assets

Depreciation refers to the process of writing-off a proportion of the value of physical assets every year of their useful life, to reflect the fact that the assets will be "used up" over a period of years.

56

The Book Values will eventually diminish to zero, even if assets are still in use. It is beyond the scope of this book to explain the different methods and tax implications of Depreciation. Suffice it to say that it is shown in the Profit and Loss account as an Expense, or annual "cost" to the business, and also in the Balance Sheet as a set-off or subtraction from the original value of each asset (see the next chapter). In the Balance Sheet however, both annual depreciation and depreciation "Accumulated" over each asset's lifetime is shown, to calculate the current, book value, or net worth of each asset.

A Summary of main points from Chapter 3.

- "Accounting" means taking financial information from those books of account and using it to explain and understand the financial position of the business.

- Double entry bookkeeping is a system of accounting in which every transaction has a corresponding positive and negative entry (debits and credits).

- To make it easier to remember, the main rule is to: **"debit the receiver and credit the giver"**.

- The Double Entry method of recording accounts builds on the maintenance of account books and relies on ledgers, or separate books of account for each type of transaction. Basically, all entries in the account books are recorded in 'ledgers'. Far greater detail and control is possible using this system. Each ledger account is a history of money values of a particular aspect of a business.

- There are three ledgers-the sales ledger, the purchases ledger and the nominal (general) ledger. The sales and purchases ledgers holds details of transactions relating to sales and purchases grouped by customer and supplier. These are known as the **Personal Ledger. The Nominal Ledger** contains impersonal accounts and is the ledger most often used by accountants to draw up trial balances.

In the next chapter, we will look at the production of the profit and loss account and the balance sheet in more detail.

****

Chapter 4

The Final Accounts

Stages 5-6-7 of the accounting cycle-Trial balances-production of financial statement and period end.

So far, we have looked at basic bookkeeping and the use of double entry accounting techniques. From the information entered into ledgers we can start to draw up final accounts. In Chapter 4, we will look at the formulation of the final accounts, looking at the trial balance, introducing the profit and loss account (now known more commonly as the Income statement), and giving examples of the layout of the accounts. We will also introduce the balance sheet.

To successfully stay in business you have to sell sufficient goods/services to generate:

i) enough revenue with which to carry on the business, i.e. cover the costs of running it; and
ii) a profit from which to draw out money to meet your personal living expenses; and

iii) perhaps enough additional profit to provide Capital to finance future growth, or to repay any capital loans from you and/or others to the business at the outset.

To successfully manage the business you need to know how all aspects of it relate to your sales, which is the underlying reason you keep accounts and build up a picture through your system of recording information, which we have covered in the previous chapters..

All this information is revealed in the process of preparing and drawing up the Final Accounts, producing the profit and loss account and a balance sheet.

One of the first steps towards the preparation of final accounts is the preparation of the Trial Balance.

The Trial Balance

A trial balance simply takes all account balances from the accounts books, summarised in the nominal ledgers and lists them in two columns, according to whether they are debit or credit balances. This is usually done on a periodic basis, such as monthly or quarterly.

A trial balance will:

- Provide a check on the accuracy of the ledger account balances - ensuring that entries have been made correctly.

- Make preparation of the final accounts easier - we can simply use the balances from the trial balance, rather than having to refer to all the individual accounts.

Example Trial balance-Peters Building Supplies Ltd-Dec 31st

	DR (£)	CR (£)
Capital	-	1000
Cash	210	-
Bank	270	-
Mortgage	-	50
Purchases	242	-
Office supplies	24	-
Sales	-	216
Creditors	-	87
Debtors	95	-
Returns in	15	-
Returns out	-	12
Carriage out	20	-
Discount allowed	8	-
Discount received	-	9
Wages	140	-
Office fixtures	350	-
Total	**1374**	**1374**

When entering transactions in the double entry accounts we see that for every entry made on the debit side of the account there will always be a credit entry made in another account for the same amount of money. When we balance off the individual accounts in the ledgers, we should therefore find that the total of all the debit balances should be exactly equal to the total of credit balances. If the totals are not the same then a mistake must have been made in the bookkeeping.

As a rule the entries for the trial balance are as follows (a good way of remembering where the entries go is to use the word PEARLS):

Type of Account	Entry
Purchases, **E**xpenses, **A**ssets	Debit
Receipts, **L**iabilities, **S**ales	Credit

Debit entries: Audit fees, carriage inwards, carriage outwards, cash, (trade) debtors, directors' fees, equipment, interest paid, investments, machinery, motor vehicle, petty cash, premises, purchases, rates, rent, returns inwards, salaries, sales ledger control account, (opening) stock, sundry expenses, wages

Credit entries: Bank loan/overdraft, capital, (trade) creditors, discount received, mortgage, profit and loss account, purchase ledger control account, rent receivable, returns outwards, sales, share capital, share premium, VAT

Both: Bank balance (would be debit if owned and credit if owed)

Final Accounts

Following on from the trial balance, the two most important final accounts that either you or your accountant will prepare are:

i) The Profit and Loss Account (income statement); and

ii) The Balance Sheet.

Together these provide an historical record of the health and behaviour of the business, reduced to and expressed in terms of money.

THE PROFIT AND LOSS ACCOUNT (Income Statement)

As the description implies it shows at a glance how much profit has been made, from a calculation of the total income from business activities minus the total expenditure incurred in running it. There will be special characteristics in the layout chosen that reflect the uniqueness of a particular business.

Below, there are two examples of a profit and loss account. The first one is more abbreviated and relates to a Limited Company and the second one, in a slightly different format gives more detail and includes depreciation and opening and closing works in progress.

Example 1. Profit and Loss account

Overleaf.

Peters Building Supplies Profit and Loss Account year ended 2019			
	Notes	**2019**	**2018**
Turnover			
Cost of sales			
Gross profit			
Administrative expenses			
Operating profit			
Other interest receivable and similar income			
Profit on ordinary activities before taxation			
Taxation on profit on ordinary activities			
Profit (Loss) for the financial year			

As you will see, example 1 shows general headings, which give a less detailed snapshot. If the P/L account is prepared by an accountant then there will be notes to the accounts, for the reader to refer to which gives detailed information about each heading.

Example 2 More detailed Profit and Loss account in a slightly different format.

Overleaf.

Peters Building Supplies Ltd Profit and Loss Account year ended 2019		
	£	£
INCOME		
Sales proceeds (Turnover)	X add Closing work in progress	
		X
Less Opening work in progress	(X)	
Bank interest receivable	X	
Less: Expenditure		
Administrative expenses	X	
Salaries/wages	X	
Business rates	X	
Light and heat	X	
Postage	X	
Telephones	X	
Stationary	X	
Etc		
Etc		
Add Accrued expenses	X	
Less Prepaid expenses	(X)	
Add Bad debts	X	
Add Depreciation of assets for year	X	(X)
Profit (Loss)	X	

NOTES TO MORE DETAILED PROFIT AND LOSS STATEMENT

i) Closing-work-in-progress. At any one time you may have done work on orders which are not yet finished. This work therefore is "in progress" and represents income earned which has not yet been invoiced. It is recognised as such in the P/L account (and also shown in the Balance sheet as a Current asset). It has to be accounted for because ultimately you will be completing the work and receiving payment, so at the moment the accounts are produced (31st March), the business is "owed" the money. Therefore you need to show Closing work-in-progress as an addition to Sales (CR) and show the same figure in the Balance Sheet as a Current Asset (DR).

ii) Opening-work-in-progress is the work that was in progress at the end of the previous accounting year and therefore must be deducted from Sales income for the year shown in these accounts. This is because it would have been invoiced and turned into Income during the year, or have become a bad debt and dealt with elsewhere in the accounts. If it were not deducted from this year's income it would have been included twice.

iii) Salaries/Wages and Light/Heat could be further separated out if there were substantial sums involved.

iv) Accrued Expenses are the total of unpaid bills outstanding at 31st March. The figure represents expenses that have been incurred during the year but not yet paid. The appropriate adjustment in the accounts is to increase the relevant expense, e.g. Telephones, in the P/L account (DR), and create a liability in the Balance Sheet (CR) to show that the sum is unpaid--as an "Accrued Expense".

v) Prepayments are expenses paid in advance of the period to which they relate, typically for such items as Insurance. Only those expenses incurred during the year can be charged to the P/L account. So any expense actually paid during this year but which relates to next year must be deducted from this year's expenses. The appropriate adjustment is to reduce the relevant expense, since it includes the amount prepaid (CR), and also create a debtor in the Balance Sheet (DR) under a separate heading of "Prepayments".

This is because if the business ceased to trade on 31st March (the Accounting Date), then any prepaid expense would have to be refunded to the business, so the prepayment is treated as a debtor.

vi) Bad Debts have been explained earlier. In summary a bad debt is an amount owing to the business for work done/goods supplied but which has not been and is not going to be paid. It therefore becomes an expense or cost to the business and must be written off.

vii) Depreciation of assets. As explained, this is a subject best left to your accountant to advise upon. Technically it represents the proportion of the value of a fixed asset that has been "used up" in the current period to help produce the profit for the year.

viii) VAT is ignored for the purposes of drawing up final accounts. It is money that "passes through" a business but is independent of its operation, since it does not "belong" to the business.

ix) Figures shown as deductions in accounts are always expressed in brackets. (x) A calculation resulting from a deduction in the left hand column is extended one line lower and is shown in the centre column ; ditto in the centre column is extended one line lower and is shown in the right hand column, if 3 columns are used.

THE BALANCE SHEET

As explained, a balance sheet is simply a list of the assets, liabilities and capital of a business at a particular point in time. We have discussed the standard accounting equation which is:

Assets-Liabilities = Capital.

Together with the Income Statement (P/L account) the Balance Sheet sets out in summary form the financial position of the business at the close of the financial year. It will show what a business has in terms of assets, what it owes in terms of liabilities and how it is financed, i.e. its capital.

Sample balance sheet, with figures added, overleaf.

Peters Building Supplies Ltd March 31st

A typical Balance Sheet layout looks as follows:		
	£	**£**
Fixed (Tangible) Assets		
Land and building at cost		54,394
Fixtures and fittings at cost		47,726
Motor vehicles at cost		50,726
Total fixed assets		**152,846**
Current assets		
Stock	36,352	
Debtors	14,263	
Prepayments	2358	
Cash at bank	532	
Total Current Assets	**53,496**	

LESS CURRENT LIABILITIES		
Bank overdraft	2846	
Creditors	27,495	
Accrued expenses	3742	
Loans	5000	
Taxes	2394	
TOTAL C/L	**41,207**	
NET CURRENT ASSETS		**12,289**
NET ASSETS		**165,135**
CAPITAL (EQUITY)		
Share Capital		1000
Profit and Loss Account (Reserves)		164,135
TOTAL CAPITAL		**165,135**

Like the P/L account, various methods of presentation layout are possible, though usually a three or four column vertical form is used to show the broad categories of information.

Considering that the Balance Sheet is the culmination of a whole financial year's bookkeeping, it is a timely reminder of the importance of regular and accurate book-keeping and the production of frequent trial balance exercises. If for example monthly trial balances have been drawn down accurately for the first ten months of the financial year, then it follows that any errors must have occurred in the final two months. In most cases this will be so. We will recall that the categories of account appearing in the Balance Sheet are the Assets and Liabilities of the business.

A) ASSETS.

These include all the items of value owned by the business, including what is owed to it. Each is shown in one of two categories as follows:

i) Fixed Assets. Those with a relatively long life which are used on a continuing basis in the activities of the business and are sometimes referred to as Tangible assets. They include freehold premises, the value of a leasehold, furniture, motor vehicles, machinery and equipment.

ii) Current Assets. These are Cash or other assets expected to be converted into cash in the near future. It is an accounting convention to show them in increasing order of "liquidity", i.e. the ease with which they are convertible into cash, the least liquid being shown first, as follows:

a) Closing Work-in-progress and/or Stock are the least liquid because you don't know when they will be converted into cash by sales.

b) Next comes Debtors (customers who have yet to pay for goods/services supplied), sometimes shown as Amounts due from Customers/Clients. From this sum will be deducted any amount assumed to be Bad Debts. Note that if a "Bad Debt" does get paid later, an adjustment must be made in the subsequent year's Balance Sheet.

c) Next in order of liquidity will be payments made in advance, or Prepayments. Think about this from the "snap shot" viewpoint, which is what the Final Accounts represents. A payment made in advance is a kind of "loan" and a refund would be due should trading cease at the end of the accounting period. Therefore it is an asset. Prepayments occur because financial periods for your insurers, for example, do not necessarily coincide with the financial year of the business, so overlap payments often occur if such payments are required in advance.

d) Next in order of liquidity is Cash at the bank.

e) Finally the most liquid of all assets is Cash in hand, represented by Petty Cash, if there is any available which is not the case with Peter..

B) LIABILITIES

From the aggregate total of Fixed and Current assets must be deducted the total Liabilities of the business at the "snap shot" date, i.e. the monies owed by the business.

Current Liabilities. Are those debts which fall to be paid within the coming 12 months. These include:

a) Bank Overdrafts
b) Trade Creditors
c) Outstanding expenses. These are running costs not yet paid, otherwise known as Accruals or Accrued expenses.

Long-term Liabilities. Those debts falling due for settlement 12 months or more after the date of the Balance Sheet. Such liabilities are usually long-term loans but exclude bank overdrafts, which can be called in at short notice at any time.

Capital (Equity)

The capital (Equity) of the business represent shareholders capital and profit and loss reserves.

Another purpose of the Balance Sheet is to provide a basis for valuing the business as an entity. Taken literally, a Balance Sheet is a sheet of the balances taken from the double entry system of bookkeeping at the end of a financial year.

The principle of Double Entry provides that in the Balance Sheet the total Assets must equal the total Capital.

The total Capital is another way of describing the sources of finance used in a business, which is another way of describing what is owed by the business to those providers of the finance.

A Summary of Main points from Chapter 4

- To successfully manage a business you need to know how all aspects of it relate to your sales, which is the underlying reason you keep accounts and build up a picture through your system of recording information.
- All this information is revealed in the process of preparing and drawing up the Final Accounts, producing the profit and loss account and a balance sheet.
- One of the first steps towards the preparation of final accounts is the preparation of the Trial Balance. A Trial balance will provide a check on the accuracy of the ledger account balances - ensuring that entries have been made correctly.
- Following on from the trial balance you will prepare a Profit and Loss Account (income statement);and a Balance Sheet. Together these provide an historical record of the health and behaviour of the business, reduced to and expressed in terms of money.

Ch.5

Accounting for VAT

In Chapter 5, we will look at how a business which is VAT registered should account for VAT, covering areas such as the VAT system, how it works, registration, goods and services and tax invoices.

A fully comprehensive guide to the complexities of the VAT system is beyond the scope of this book and only a brief outline will be provided. Suffice to say that if you are registered for VAT with HM Revenue and Customs then you are liable to account to that authority for VAT passing through your books. In effect you are an unpaid tax collector.

Your local VAT office will advise you on all VAT matters and enquiries regarding VAT administration. Do not neglect to seek advice from HMRC and/or your accountant before you commence business, because:

a) the best advice will depend upon the circumstances of your business; and

b) you will not be excused by HM Revenue and Customs for failing to get advice. They will presume you have been so advised on how the system works and what you have to do; and

c) the system is complex.

The VAT system

Value Added Tax is defined as the tax chargeable on the supply of goods or services, where the supply is a taxable supply and made by a taxable person in the course of business carried on by him/her. The taxable person is the one who is liable to account to HM Revenue and Customs for the amount of tax charged on the supply of goods/services.

A **"Business"**-When are you in business and when are you not? "Business" can have a very wide meaning and includes the way in which self-employed individuals earn income by way of trade, vocation or profession. HM Revenue and Customs define business as "any continuing activity which is mainly concerned with making supplies to other persons for a consideration".

Supply of Goods-This means a supply that transfers the exclusive ownership of the goods to someone else.

Supply of Services-This means doing something (except supplying goods), and receiving in return what the law calls a "consideration". This means any kind of payment - monetary or otherwise, and includes something which is also a supply. So a "consideration" to the business in return for the business making a supply includes anything given to cover the costs of making the supply.

Taxable Supply-This means any supply of goods/services except an exempt supply. A list of exempt supplies can be obtained from your local VAT Office or online at HMRC.gov.uk

Taxable supplies are of two kinds:

i) Those chargeable at the Standard rate (currently 20%).

(ii)Those chargeable at a zero rate. Zero rated supplies include water, books and periodicals, and food not consumed on premises but which is sold for outside consumption.

Exempt and Zero-rated supplies are similar because no VAT is actually charged in either case to a customer. However, you must be aware of the crucial difference between the two because only a registered business that makes a Taxable supply can reclaim VAT paid for supplies to that business. Zero rated supplies are taxable supplies. If your business makes Zero rated supplies it is a "Taxable Person" for VAT purposes. This means that VAT can be claimed back on purchases made by a business that is zero rated, if it is registered.

Exempt supplies are **not** taxable supplies. If your business only makes Exempt supplies it is not a "Taxable Person" for VAT purposes and therefore VAT paid on purchases by the business cannot be reclaimed from HMRC. There are special and complex rules about partial exemption applicable to suppliers of exempt goods/services (health operations, financial services and a few others). If you believe your business might qualify then contact your local VAT office. Briefly the size, type and level of business determine whether your business qualifies for partial exemption.

It should be clear by now that VAT can apply to your business even if the turnover is quite modest, because it is inevitable that VAT is going to be paid on purchases, regardless of whether it is charged on sales.

Discounts on Taxable Supplies

If you intend to offer discounts on products or services, as many businesses do, you need to know the VAT position on this kind of sale. There are two kinds of discount in operation in business.

a) An unconditional discount to a customer naturally means that s/he will pay the asking price less the discount. VAT is charged on the lower price because that is the asking price, the one the buyer will accept.

b) A conditional discount is one where a lower price will operate provided that the buyer pays promptly within a specified discount period, e.g. 14 days. In this case VAT is charged on the lower, discounted sum even if the customer does not pay within the specified discount period.

The tax value of the supply is the value of what is provided on which VAT is charged, because the lower sum will be at least the minimum amount paid for the purchase, assuming that the buyer takes advantage of the discounted price.

Time of Supply

The time at which a supply is made is known as the Tax Point. It is important because it begins the period at the end of which a taxable business becomes liable to account for tax charged on a taxable supply.

Generally the Tax Point for the sale of goods is when the goods are given over to the purchaser, which of course may not be when they are paid for, as in a credit sale. The Tax Point for services is when the services are completed, which again may not be the same time as when they are paid for.

The most important exceptions are:

i) If a tax invoice is issued within 14 days after the basic tax point, the invoice date will be the tax point for the purpose of fixing the beginning of the quarterly period of account in which the VAT on it becomes liable for payment to HM R&C, unless a longer period is agreed.

ii) If payment is received, or a tax invoice rendered before the basic tax point arises, then the supply will be treated as occurring at the date the payment was made, or the date the invoice was rendered.

REGISTRATION

A) Compulsory

If you anticipate that the sales income of the business in the current trading year will reach the threshold level prescribed by law, (you can gain information on current thresholds by contacting HMRC) you must contact your local VAT office and inform them that the business is liable for registration for VAT.

Upon registration the business will be allotted a unique Registration number, which must be shown on all business stationery.

VAT must then be charged on all sales the business makes, whether on credit or for cash, at the prescribed rate, except on those goods/services which are either zero-rated or exempt. This is called the Output Tax.

The VAT paid by the business on purchases of materials etc. is called the Input tax.

HMRC must be paid the amount of VAT charged by the business on sales (**whether collected within the relevant quarter or not**) minus the VAT paid by the business on its purchases. This is normally done at the end of each quarter, though a longer time period can sometimes be negotiated.

Retail businesses, i.e. those selling to the public, do not need to render VAT invoices unless a buyer requests one.

HM R&C publish a number of leaflets and notices explaining in great detail all you need to know about VAT and your business, as a sole trader, partnership or limited company. Among the most important are:

l) VAT Notice 700: The VAT Guide. In fact a booklet of more than 140 pages.

ii) "Should I register for VAT?" This Guide (700/1) is vital because HMRC will impose financial penalties for failure to register when you should and also for late payments.

iii) "Filling in your VAT Return". A useful guide on what format to adopt and how to present VAT Return forms.

If you believe that you are not obliged to register, because turnover will remain below the threshold, you should still consider the issue carefully. There are circumstances when you can reclaim VAT incurred before registration, if you then register at a later date. For example, VAT paid on vans (but not cars) and stock can later be reclaimed, disregarding the time of purchase, so long as the items are for business use. Of course you must produce VAT invoices to evidence the amount reclaimed.

If you engage the services of either solicitors or estate agents to set up the business, then VAT on their fee invoices can be reclaimed if they were incurred up to 6 months before the business was registered.

b) Voluntary

Compulsory registration arises simply because of the proximity of your turnover to the threshold level.

As an alternative you may want to consider voluntary registration, even if your turnover is substantially below the threshold level for compulsory registration.

The advantage is of course that Input tax paid on purchases subject to VAT can then be reclaimed.

The disadvantage is that VAT will have to be charged on the taxable supplies made by the business, which could well affect the competitiveness of your products/services. If competitors are not charging VAT and you are this might present a serious problem.

If the business is not registered, compulsorily or voluntarily, then it will have to bear the incidence of Input tax paid. You will have to consider whether the business can absorb this cost or whether you need to raise the selling prices.

Tax Invoices

A) Inputs to the Business

Once registered, tax invoices are important because they evidence your right to recover Input tax on supplies made to the business by a supplier who is also registered. Without tax invoices you will not be able to claim a deduction of the VAT paid.

B) Outputs of the Business

If you have registered the business then you are compelled to charge VAT on sales, whether on credit or for cash. Furthermore, tax invoices can only be raised if the business is VAT registered, and not otherwise.

As a matter of good business practice it is best to quote a VAT-inclusive price to customers. The current rate is significantly high and could have a serious impact on the cash flows of your own business and that of your suppliers, because most registered persons and businesses are locked in to the quarterly Return cycle.

Assuming the business is registered, and is therefore a taxable person, then within 30 days of making a physical taxable supply, the customer must be provided with a tax invoice.

As we saw from our example invoice in chapter 2, every Tax Invoice must by law state the following particulars:-

a) An invoice number, for identification purposes

b) The date of the supply, ie the tax point

c) The name, address and VAT registration number of the business

d) The name and address of the person to whom the sale has been made

e) The kind of supply that has been made, e.g. sale, hire

f) An adequate description of the goods or services supplied

g) The precise quantity of goods supplied or the extent of the services provided and separate amounts payable under each heading

h) The total amount payable and a breakdown of separate amounts against each item, if more than one

i) Details of any discount allowable for prompt cash payment

j) The rate of tax applicable and the amount of tax charged.

If upon inspection invoices do not satisfy HMRC requirements then you put at risk your ability to reclaim input tax. Bear in mind that HMRC have authority to inspect all your books and records relating to VAT at any time, with or without your co-operation.

An additional aid to VAT invoice monitoring is a simple invoice record, listing all invoices raised in number sequences and with separate analysis columns providing for arithmetic calculation of output VAT and net sales.

Tax collection

As noted previously, accounting for VAT is almost always to quarterly accounting periods. With permission from HMRC you may want to opt for an annual accounting scheme, where one tax return is made at the end of the year and the tax liability paid by direct debit in nine monthly instalments of amounts agreed with HMRC.

Within one month after the end of a tax quarter, a completed return form and a cheque for the tax due, or a BACS payment, must be sent to HMRC. There are penalties for late payment.

The Statutory return form provided by your local VAT office must detail the amount payable and how that sum has been calculated, i.e., the total output tax charges less the total input tax deductible. The return must also detail the VAT exclusive values of all sales and purchases made and incurred. The leaflet accompanying the form shows you exactly how to set this information out.

Bad debt relief

As noted previously, it is possible that your business will incur a bad debt, from time to time. The amount to be written off can include VAT if the invoice raised was a VAT invoice. Relief can be claimed for the VAT element of a bad debt which is more than six months old and has been written off in your accounts. If the debt is subsequently paid then naturally you must refund the VAT portion of the debt, whether recovered in whole or in part.

Accounting for VAT in your books

You are required to keep records of all taxable supplies and receipts of taxable goods and services made in the course of business. This includes standard, zero rated and exempt supplies. If your methods of keeping these records create problems for HMRC in any audit exercise they carry out they have power to direct necessary changes to your procedures. All VAT records must be kept for six years and can only be disposed of with the permission of HMRC. We have already examined how to highlight the VAT element in your book of accounts.

****

Ch. 6

Accounting for Limited Companies

Throughout the book we have concentrated on bookkeeping and accounts for business of all types, with the exception of Public Limited Companies (PLC's), which are the subject of another book as they are far more complex.

In Chapter 6, we will take a look at the Limited Company in more detail as this is the most common form of business entity and also involves the use of share capital..

The limited liability company

The modern type of limited company came into being, or common use, during the latter part of the nineteenth century. Before the advent of limited companies the main form of trading vehicle had been the sole proprietorship or partnership. However, this type of vehicle became unsuitable when outside investors began putting in capital and buying shares in the company.

This is the main reason for the formation of limited companies, so that an investor, or investors who put up capital for a venture without being involved in the management will only have that limited amount of capital at risk, rather than having unlimited liability against all their personal wealth.

A Limited Company is a legal entity-legal 'person' in it's own right and can be sued for breach of contract, debts owed and other matters. However, it is a different 'person' from the shareholder or director, and neither can, in principle, be required to pay money owed by the company. The law and accounting procedures governing a limited company rely on the main principle that ownership and management are two entirely different functions.

Limited companies-owners of the company and managers

The owners of a limited company are the shareholders and their entitlement to a share of profits in a company depends on the amount of their shareholding. Shares normally carry voting rights, again in proportion to the amount owned. The shareholders meet in annual meetings and will elect directors to manage the company on their behalf. Directors are managers of the company and are distinct from directors.

Financial statements

The role of financial statements is crucial in that it allows the shareholders, who are not involved in the day to day management of the company, to see how managers are carrying out their job. Because of this requirement there are detailed statutory rules on how the accounts of a limited company should be set out. These rules are contained in the Companies Acts, the most recent being the Companies Act 2006. In addition to the basic accounting requirements, limited companies may have to have an annual audit, which entails an outside check of their accounts. Smaller companies are not required to have an audit, but in certain circumstances, depending on the business, may be required to have one.

Limited company capital

The constitution and rules of a company are contained within two documents called the Memorandum of Association and the Articles of Association. These set out the types of share capital the company is entitled to issue, and the rules governing the voting of shareholders and the relationship of shareholders to the company. In the simplest type of capital structure, a company has the right to issue a given number of ordinary shares, called the authorised share capital, which it has actually issued to shareholders who have paid the full price of the share to the company.

Shares give the shareholder a right to receive a share of the profits, but only when it is agreed between shareholders to distribute them. This distribution is called a dividend and will be declared as so much per share. the decision whether or not to pay a dividend is taken at an Annual General meeting (AGM), although in practice it s usually the directors who decide how much is to be paid out by proposing a dividend payout for the year that the shareholders then ratify as part of the AGM. Shares can be bought and sold freely. They are only worth what someone is prepared to pay for them. Unless they are specifically issued as redeemable shares they need never be repaid by the company. We have all seen, during the process of takeovers, how the company or individual wishing to take over a company will offer a premium on the share price to persuade shareholders to sell.

Loan capital

In addition to raising money by issuing shares in a company, capital can also be raised in the form of a loan. Money can be borrowed. Sometimes this is from a bank, other times certificates are issued, known as debentures or loan stock. These certificates usually carry a fixed rate of interest and the right to have the capital repaid at a certain time. For example, a company might issue £20,000 7% debentures, redeemable in 2018. This means that, on receipt of the £20,000 every year until 2018 the company must pay £1600 and in 2018 the £20,000 must be repaid.

Characteristics of limited company accounts

It is important to understand the differences between the financial statements of a limited company and a sole trader.

There are two main areas of difference between financial statements of a sole trader and those of a limited company.- what happens after net profit in the profit and loss account, and what is shown in capital on the balance sheet.

Having calculated net profit as for sole proprietors, this is taken down to an appropriation account, which shows how the profit is to be appropriated.

The first element to be deducted is corporation tax, to give profit after tax. next, any balance brought forward from previous years is added. The dividends proposed on the shares are then deducted, and finally a balance of profit brought forward is left. It is illegal for a company to distribute more than it has in total profit, both earned in the year and brought forward.

Example

Limited company appropriation account		
Net profit		
	£20,000	
Less corporation tax	£4,800	
	_____	
	£15,200	add retained
profit brought forward		
	£6000	
	_____	
	£21,200	
Less dividend proposed		
	£10,000	
Retained profit c/f		
	£11,200	

On the balance sheet, the share capital appears separately from the brought forward profits, but all of them are still shareholders funds. the brought forward profits are sometimes called reserves.

Accounting for share capital

Registered and issued share capital

The nominal, authorised or registered share capital is that stated in the company's Memorandum of Association. That part of the authorised share capital which is issued to the public is shown under the heading of issued capital on the balance sheet in the below manner.

Authorised and issued share capital		
Authorised capital	£	£
50,000 preference shares of £1 each	50,000	
300,000 ordinary shares of 50p each	£150,000	£200,000
	———	———
Issued capital		
50,000 8% preference shares of £1 each	£50,000	
fully paid		
200,000 ordinary shares at 50p each	£100,000	£150,000
fully paid		

Note that it is only the issued share capital that forms part of the double entry system, and consequently the authorised capital is ruled off when it is not yet issued. There are various categories of capital. In the figures shown above, the nominal, registered or authorised capital is £200,000. the issued capital is £150,000, consisting of 50,000 8% shares, fully paid up and 200,000 ordinary shares of 50p fully paid up. the uncalled capital of 50,000 has yet to be issued.

There are also various classes of shares, the two main classes being preference and ordinary. the former carries a fixed rate of interest, which is payable before the payment of any dividends to shareholders.

Share issues

With some public share issues, payments for shares taken up may be made by instalments. A new company may be floated with an authorised share capital of 100,000 ordinary shares of £1 each. half the registered capital is to be offered to the general public and is to be paid in three distinct stages:

20p on application by 25th April
30p on allotment on 25th June
50p first and final call on 1st August.

The build up of the company's finances is now shown over these three months and the ordinary share capital is built up in this way, via application, allotment and final call accounts. The liability of a company member is limited to the amount that he or she paid for the shareholding. If he has not paid all the 'calls' made on him by the company, he becomes a debtor for the money that is due. Sums owed by a defaulting shareholder are known as 'calls in arrear'.

Premiums on shares

A successful company, perhaps needing further capital for expansion, might put out an additional issue of shares at a premium, i.e. an amount above the nominal or par value of the shares. If, for instance, the nominal value of the shares was £1 and they were issued at £1.20 a share, the premium would be 20%. An applicant for 100 shares would pay £120 for them.

The Companies Act requires amounts received as premiums on shares to be taken to a share premium account as a capital reserve. This kind of reserve can only be used for a special purpose (such as offsetting capital losses) and is not available for transfer to the credit of the revenue account and to be used as payment for a dividend, as in the case of a general reserve.

The final accounts of a limited company

The 'published section' of the profit and loss account

The companies Act 1985 provides a rigid hierarchy of headings which must be used in reporting the results of a limited company. the main headings for a profit and loss account for example, begin as follows:

- ➢ Turnover
- ➢ Cost of sales
- ➢ Gross profit or loss
- ➢ Distribution costs
- ➢ Administrative expenses.

The Companies Acts also require full public disclosure of certain items which are normally included as notes. Full details must be given of directors fees and salaries, loan and debenture interest, and the depreciation of fixed assets. Information must also be given of the following 'appropriation' of profit:

➤ Amounts paid or reserved for taxation

➤ Dividends paid or recommended

➤ Amounts transferred to, or withdrawn from, reserves.

The purpose of these disclosures is for the benefit of shareholders, creditors, debenture holders and HMRC.

Balance sheet disclosures

The format for the balance sheet is equally rigid, for example with fixed assets normally forming the opening item, split into intangible, tangible and investments, and each of these further divided into four or more categories.

Overall, there are fundamental differences between accounts for limited companies and those of a sole trader, essentially because of the issue and use of share capital, corporation tax and payment of dividends.

****

Summary of main points from Chapter 6

- The main reason for the formation of limited companies is that an investor, or investors who puts up capital for a venture without being involved in the management will only have that limited amount of capital at risk, rather than having unlimited liability against all their personal wealth.

- The law and accounting procedures governing a limited company rely on the main principle that ownership and management are two entirely different functions.

- The owners of a limited company are the shareholders and their entitlement to a share of profits in a company depends on the amount of their shareholding.

- There are two main areas of difference between financial statements of a sole trader and those of a limited company.-what happens after net profit in the profit and loss account, and what is shown in capital on the balance sheet

****

Chapter 7

How the Tax System Operates in the UK and Tax Deadlines

How the tax system works

In the United Kingdom, as in most other countries, the government raises taxes and spends these taxes in accordance with economic policies. Taxes can be levied by local authorities in addition to government. The UK tax year runs from 6th of April to 5th of April the following year. If you are self- employed then your accounting year does not have to run for the same period and you can select any date you want. Most people use the actual formal tax year because it is easier to administer.

Each year there is an annual budget, delivered in Spring and there is also an Autumn statement, which is an interim statement of how things are in relation to the annual budget and the nations finances generally. Currently, in 2018 the situation is that the Chancellor has announced one budget per annum instead of two.

HMRC

HM Revenue and Customs (HMRC) are responsible for the collection of all taxes except for rates and council tax. HMRC also administers tax credits, the minimum wage, statutory sick pay, maternity pay, paternity and adoption pay and student loans. Therefore HMRC has a wide remit.

Assessment of taxes-Self Assessment

Individuals are responsible for self-assessing their own tax and National Insurance liabilities and also payments of any loans. This is achieved by filling in an annual tax return. Individuals are usually notified that they must complete a tax return. The return can either be sent by post or more likely online-the dates being 31st October for paper returns and 31st January for online filing. You'll need to send a tax return if, in the last tax year:

- you were self-employed - you can deduct allowable expenses
- you got £2,500 or more in untaxed income, for example from renting out a property or savings and investments
- your savings or investment income was £10,000 or more before tax
- you made profits from selling things like shares, a second home or other chargeable assets and need to pay Capital Gains Tax
- you were a company director - unless it was for a non-profit organisation (such as a charity) and you didn't get any pay or benefits, like a company car
- your income (or your partner's) was over £50,000 and one of you claimed Child Benefit

- you had income from abroad that you needed to pay tax on
- you lived abroad and had a UK income
- you got dividends from shares and you're a higher or additional rate taxpayer
- your income was over £100,000
- you were a trustee of a trust or registered pension scheme
- you had a P800 from HMRC saying you didn't pay enough tax last year - and you didn't pay what you owe through your tax code or with a voluntary payment

Certain other people may need to send a return (for example religious ministers or Lloyd's underwriters) - you can check whether you need to. You usually won't need to send a return if your only income is from your wages or pension.

If you've been told to send a return

If you get an email or letter from HM Revenue and Customs telling you to send a return, you must send it - even if you don't have any tax to pay. If you used to send a tax return but don't need to send one for the last tax year, you can contact HMRC to close your Self- Assessment account. You must also tell HMRC if you've stopped being self-employed.

Claiming tax relief

Fill in a tax return to claim money back from HMRC for:

- donations to charity
- private pension contributions as a higher or additional rate taxpayer, or if your scheme isn't set up for automatic tax relief
- work expenses over £2,500

Registering for Self-Assessment

You need to register if you didn't send a tax return last year. How you do this depends on whether:

- you're self-employed
- you need to sebd a return for another reason

If you're new to Self-Assessment, you'll need to keep records (for example bank statements or receipts) so you can fill in your tax return correctly.

Companies

For limited companies, the period covered by your return will be your accounting period as opposed to the tax year. So if your tax year runs from 1st November to October 30th your tax return will run from this date. The corporation tax return must be filed within 12 months of the end of the company's tax period. All company forms have to be filed electronically.

All employers are required to provide details of National Insurance and other deductions that they take from employees, each time they run a payroll. This is called Real Time Information.

Keeping records

If you are self-employed you need to keep your records for five years and ten months from the end of the tax year. For limited companies you are required to maintain records for 6 years. PAYE and CIS (Construction Industry records) must be kept for three years in addition to the current tax year. If you fail to keep these records then you can be fined by HMRC.

Companies must complete an annual return form (CT600) and file it online, together with accounts and tax computations. HMRC can advise on completion. You should go to their website www.hmrc.gov/ukct/managing/company-tax-return/index.htm.

Inaccurate or late returns

If you make an honest error you can correct this as you go, or later by following a set procedure. However, if you file an inaccurate return deliberately or carelessly you can be fined. If you have filed your return late you will receive automatic penalties. The scale of the penalty will depend on the lateness of the return. Details of fines can be found on the HMRC website.

HMRC compliance checks

HMRC can check all supporting documents and will do so if they believe that there is a problem with tax return information. They will also randomly check tax returns. HMRC will give you notice of an enquiry. You can appeal against the outcome of a compliance check.

The Range of Taxes a Business is Liable For

Having considered the operation of the tax system we need to move on to understanding the range of taxes that businesses are responsible for so that you have a clear picture of your potential liabilities.

You will find that there are two (main) types of taxes raised in the UK, direct taxes and indirect taxes. Income will be taxed directly along with profits and any capital gains. **Direct taxes** can be grouped into four categories:

- Income tax
- Inheritance tax paid by the individual
- Corporation tax paid by companies
- Capital gains tax paid by both individuals and companies

In addition to taxes there will be liability for National Insurance. All employers will be liable for Class 1 employer's contributions based on the wages and salary paid to employees including directors.

Indirect taxes are those taxes charged on items of expenditure and include VAT, other excise duties and any stamp duties in addition to industry specific taxes such as power generation, transport and banking.

HM Revenue and Customs are responsible for collection and repayment of taxes. Local authorities will collect other taxes such as council tax and business rates.

Calculation of income tax for sole traders

There are a number of steps to follow when working out your liability for tax if you are a **sole trader**, as follows:

Deduct your personal allowance from your income-everyone has a personal allowance which increases each year-for 2019/2020 it is £12.500. If your income in 2019/20 exceeds £100,000 then your allowances will be restricted. Basically, for every £2 over £100,000 your personal allowance goes down by £1. After you have deducted your personal allowance the first tranche of your income will be taxed at the basic rate of 20% from thereon the rates are as set out in appendix one.

Companies and Corporation Tax

As explained, the tax situation for limited companies is somewhat different to that of self-employed. Corporation tax is a tax paid by companies on their profits, and also any capital gains, during the financial year. The profits of a company will take into account all sources of income, including income from any investments and also from property, such as rents. There are differences in the way company profits are calculated, to those of a sole trader and partners. For example, companies, but not sole traders or partners can claim a tax deduction for expenditure on goodwill and intangible assets and other allowances, such as research and development, depending on their trade.

If a company is a member of a group of companies, it is taxed on its own profits but groups are treated differently from individual companies in certain respects, including treatment of losses. For certain, if you are operating a group of companies you will need specialist accounting.

Essentially, Corporation Tax is charged on the profits of all UK resident companies and also non-resident companies that trade in the UK through agencies or branches.

The payment of Dividends by a Limited Company

If your company pays a dividend, there is no tax to pay on that dividend but the dividend is not a tax deductible expense in calculating your corporation tax bill. Dividends are paid with a 10% tax credit and unless the recipient is a higher or additional rate tax payer there is no further income tax to pay on the dividend. Dividends are also not liable to National Insurance. Dividends which the company receives are not liable to corporation tax.

Capital gains tax

Capital Gains Tax is a tax paid by individuals (sole traders and partners) and by companies on the profit when you sell (or 'dispose of') something (an 'asset') that's increased in value. It's the gain you make that's taxed, not the amount of money you receive. Some assets are tax-free. You also don't have to pay Capital Gains Tax if all your gains in a year are under your tax-free allowance. Disposing of an asset includes:

- selling it

- giving it away as a gift, or transferring it to someone else
- swapping it for something else
- getting compensation for it - like an insurance payout if it's been lost or destroyed

You pay Capital Gains Tax on the gain when you sell (or 'dispose of'):

- most personal possessions worth £6,000 or more, apart from your car
- property that isn't your main home
- your main home if you've let it out, used it for business or it's very large
- shares that aren't in an ISA or PEP
- business assets

These are known as 'chargeable assets'.Depending on the asset, you may be able to reduce any tax you pay by claiming a relief. If you dispose of an asset you jointly own with someone else, you have to pay Capital Gains Tax on your share of the gain. You don't usually pay tax on gifts to your husband, wife, civil partner or a charity. You don't pay Capital Gains Tax on certain assets, including any gains you make from:

- ISAs or PEPs
- UK government gilts and Premium Bonds
- Betting, lottery or pools winnings
- Transactions between spouses and partners

- Cars and other machinery and assets with a useful life of less than 50 years (but not where capital allowances have been claimed)
- Shares in Enerprise Schemes or SEED enterpise if held for at least three years
- A disposal by a trading company of a substantial shareholding (10% plus) in another
- Personal items sold for less than £6,000
- Assets passed on death
- Most life insurance proceeds

Capital Gains Tax allowances

You only have to pay Capital Gains Tax on your overall gains above your tax-free allowance (called the Annual Exempt Amount). The tax-free allowance 2019/2020 is:

- £12,000
- £6000 for trusts

Inheritance Tax is a tax on the estate (the property, money and possessions) of someone who's died. There's normally no Inheritance Tax to pay if:

- the value of your estate is below the £325,000 threshold
- you leave everything to your spouse or civil partner, a charity or a community amateur sports club

If you're married or in a civil partnership and your estate is worth less than £325,000, you can transfer any unused threshold to your partner when you die. This means their threshold can be as much as £650,000.

NATIONAL INSURANCE

You will pay National Insurance (NI) if you are self-employed, employed, a partner, employer and by all who wish to protect their contributions so that they receive full state pension. Young people under 16 do not have to pay NI and those in full time education between 16-18 also do not have to pay as they are credited with contributions during that period. If you do not work because you are looking after children or severley diabled relatives for more than 20 hours per week, you will be entitled to a weekly credit.

National Insurance classes

The class you pay depends on your employment status and how much you earn, and whether you have any gaps in your National Insurance record.

National Insurance class	Who pays (2019-2020)
Class 1	Employees earning more than £166 a week and under State Pension age - they're automatically deducted by your employer

National Insurance class	Who pays (2019-2020)
Class 1A or 1B	Employers pay these directly on their employee's expenses or benefits
Class 2	Self-employed people - you don't have to pay if you earn less than £6365 a year (but you can choose to pay voluntary contributions)
Class 3	Voluntary contributions - you can pay them to fill or avoid gaps in your National Insurance record
Class 3A	Voluntary contribution - you may be able to top up your pension with a single lump sum if you're due to retire before 6 April 2016
Class 4	Self-employed people earning profits over £8,362 a year

Payment of National Insurance

Class 1 National Insurance is collected through PAYE. Class 2 and 3 contributions are paid by monthly direct debit to the National Insurance Contributions Office (NICO) part of HMRC. Class 4 is collected through the self-assessment tax return as part of the sole traders or partners tax bill.

If you are self-employed or a partner you can claim small earnings exemption, which exempts you from paying Class 2 contributions if you expect your trading profits to fall below a certain threshold (£6365 2019/20).

If you are both self-employed and employed in the same year you may pay Class 1 NI on your employed income and Class 4 contributions on your self-employed income. The amounts paid by you may be capped as there is a maximum annual limit on the amounts to be paid. Irrespective of the number of self-employments you have you need only pay one lot of Class 2 contributions. Different amounts apply to Class 4 contributions. Here, the profits from all of your self-employments must be added together to calculate your liability.

****

PART 2: MANAGEMENT AND CONTROL

Chapter 8.

Management Accounting

In the next two chapters, we will move away from the keeping of books and accounts and into the area of using accounts as a management tool to control and develop a business.

We will concentrate on managing cash flow and formulating budgets, giving examples as we go and also look at the use of key ratios, derived from accounts, in business management.

Accurate forecasting, through the formulation of budgets and monitoring of cash flow is absolutely essential to the profitability of any business. In the previous chapters, we have seen how to develop and maintain books of account. In the following chapters we will look more closely at the process of budgeting in small businesses and at more precise control of cash flows. Profitability of a business is the outcome of two elements

- control of overheads
- correct pricing to ensure that the margin of profit is realistic.

Cash-flow

A smooth and regular cash flow, or the achievement of such involves:

- Making sure that a business is run profitably
- Payment control
- Utilisation of any available credit. This is of the utmost importance as the alternative is costly borrowing
- The attainment of correct stocking levels

Basically, money is vital to the life of any business and the forecasting of cash flow is essential in order to both measure the growth and direction of the business and to enable you to make strategic decisions at a given point in time. It is equally vital to ensure that sources of business finance are identified and readily available in times of increased need for capital.

Budgets

A budget is used, in both business and personal sense, as a tool to forecast expenditure and to monitor cash flow at regular intervals. It is a plan expressed in quantitative terms and should be part of an ongoing business plan. Budgets are necessary to enable you to plan what your business will do at given points of time. All aspects of a business have to be defined and factored into a budget, which will usually run for the financial year of the business and be broken down into monthly elements in order to allow for an ongoing review of progress. An effective budget is also essential as a tool to enable you to deal with potential funders, such as bank managers.

The monitoring function of a carefully prepared budget can help you to identify certain trends and needs, such as the maintenance of stock levels, debtors at these processes further on in the book.

An effective budget is both a guesstimate and, in certain areas, an accurate appraisal of expenditure.

Formulating budgets

Budgets are effective tools, in forecasting the pattern of business and also as a tool for development. For budgets to be of any real use they should be split up into monthly periods. As the months pass any adjustments can be made in the light of variations and can be fed into the ongoing budget. The putting together of a detailed budget involves a process which is linked.

Cash flow considerations

Central to any budget setting is the need to estimate cash flow and to ensure that your projections are adequately sourced. It is no good having a production budget which anticipates an increase of 50% in production if the money is not there to finance it. We will be looking at cash flows a little later on.

As we have seen, it is necessary to split the budget into periods of one month in order to account for variations or fluctuations in the process. This is very important if the nature of your business is affected by seasonal trends. To re-cap, the key steps involved in budget preparation are as follows:

- The period that should be covered by your budget has to be ascertained. Usually, the period will correspond to the financial year of a business. It is also necessary to decide the periods into which the budget will be divided, i.e. 12 monthly periods

- Forecast activity levels and the income from trading and other sources for each of the periods. The forecast should reflect the fact that income streams may be irregular, as is the nature for some businesses

- When the level of sales has been determined for each period it is then necessary to ascertain the cost of sales

- The next step is to forecast the level of each of the overhead expenses.

- Finally, confirm that your plan fits into the cash budget.

Having arrived at the figures you will be in a position to produce a monthly budgeted profit and loss account like the one shown overleaf. The budget will have an actuals column and also a budget column. This will enable you to see, on a monthly basis, the level of expenditure and the deviation from the budget. If there are significant variations between the actual and budget column then there will be several considerations:

- It is essential to consider why the business is not performing as you have forecasted. Where are things going wrong, if they are going wrong

- The budget may need to be revised for the rest of the year, based on the variations, which may involve management decisions related to expenditure

As we will see, this procedure of review is extended automatically to the cash flow forecast. There are key considerations for any one involved in budget setting. These are as follows:

- The quality and accuracy of any budget will depend on the assumptions made by the person/people involved in the budget process. Do not be sloppy and lazy when it comes to forecasting.
- Be rigorous and honest in your assumptions. The most important thing to realise when setting the budget is that, in a lot of cases, it will be essential to study the previous year's performance in order to be able to set a future budget.
- The budget is very much a management tool and the performance against budget at the end of each period is a crucial indicator for the future.
- Cash is the lifeblood-business activity totally depends on it and it is vital that this side is under control.
- The activities of one particular period in time will reflect and modify the next period.

*

Example budget

Items	January		February	
	Budget	Actual	Budget	Actual
Sales				
Direct costs				
Purchases of goods				
Wages				
Stock				
Cost of goods sold				
Gross profit				
Overheads				
Motor expenses				
Repairs and renewals				
Telephone charges				
Printing and stationary				
Heating and lighting				
Insurance				
Rates				
Bank charges and interest				
Professional fees				
Sundry expenses				
Depreciation				
Net profit				

The budget and its success will form your business model and should be treated with the utmost respect and consideration.

Budgeting and costs

The format of a budget should, broadly, follow the profit and loss account, although it will also include items of a capital nature. The preparation of any budget will usually be more detailed than the profit and loss account.

Costs involved in business

Some expenses in business are fixed and some are variable. There are also direct and indirect costs involved in the production process. Most direct costs are variable whilst the indirect costs are usually fixed. Direct costs are those associated with the production of the product itself whilst indirect costs are concerned with the overall running of a business.

Fixed and variable costs

If we look at the elements of fixed and variable costs, then it can be seen that raw materials to produce a product will be variable. The higher the level of overall activity the more variable the material costs. Energy for production will correspondingly vary as will transport. The logic is that the more that a business produces the more variable will the overall costs be.

However, other costs, such as rent or rates and business rates will not vary with the highs and lows of production. These costs will remain stable, they will be the same even if you did not produce a thing. The costs of salaries are fixed and identifiable and are therefore fixed.

Semi-variable costs

Some costs are not regarded as truly variable. Key examples may be labour and machinery. When production reaches a certain limit it may be necessary to take on more labour and invest in more machinery. This will obviously come into effect with increased production and this is why labour and machinery has to be identified as semi-variable in nature. Particular attention should be paid to this area as incorrect forecasting can have a detrimental effect on business planning.

Selling expenses

The size of a sales force will clearly be affected by the levels of activity within the business. If interest is shown in a product then it may be necessary to increase your sales force, if appropriate. This is also a consideration to take on board.

Budgeting sales income

The top line on the profit and loss account is usually the sales income. Very often it is the sales figure that heads the budget and everything else is fitted in. If you have been in business for a while then past trends can influence your future budget. It will be essential to look at the number of units sold and also the values of those units. The unit values decided upon by yourself will very much reflect the type of business that you are engaged in. For example, a publisher would measure units in terms of individual books, a window cleaner individual houses and so on.

120

Who should carry out the sales forecasting

If you work alone then the answer is simple-you will do the forecasting. If the organisation is larger then all departments will usually have a hand in the forecasting process. It is absolutely essential that the process is well coordinated.

Creating the budget

From research carried out you have identified that the sales of your product will be along the following lines:

Product	Unit sales per month
Books-paperback	750
Books-hardback	350
Magazines	450

The prices of the products are likely to be:	
	£
Books-paperback	7 .99
Books-hardback	9.99
Magazines	3.50

Therefore the monthly sales figures would look like this:			
Product	Units	Price	Value
		£	£
Books-paperback	750	7.99	5992.50
Books hardback	350	9.99	3496.50
Magazines	450	3.50	1575
		Value	**11064**

If your business has seasonal trends then it will be necessary to produce separate figure for each month in order to maintain an accurate picture.

Arriving at price-price budgeting

You will usually have a keen idea of the market and corresponding prices for your goods. However, you also need to sell your goods at a profit and you therefore need to establish how much the product has cost in order to ascertain your profit margins. When trying to establish the actual cost of production it is necessary to take into account the fact that there are two types of cost-direct and indirect costs. As we have seen, direct costs are those incurred directly in producing the product and they include materials, wages and other direct costs such as energy.

Indirect costs are those costs which do not relate directly to production, including costs of selling and marketing, rent, rates and insurance.

Example - Direct and indirect costs

Overleaf.

Direct and Indirect costs	
Direct Costs	Indirect costs
Materials	Overheads
+	Admin + labour
Direct Labour	Selling and marketing
+	Insurance-building
repairs	
Production costs	Depreciation
	Proportion

COST OF ITEM

Having projected your sales and anticipated income, then you will need to set this off against the actual costs of production. Remember the actual cost of production will include all costs, direct and indirect. Therefore, if you are producing books, and you both manufacture and sell the product and the out-turn price of a paperback is £7.99, this will be set off against the actual costs of production. For example:

Costs of production

Product-Paperback book

Print run 1000

Materials required

	£
Paper 100 mts	Cost 1 50
Cover film	Cost 100

Bar code   Cost 9.99

Glue   Cost 20.00

                                          Total 279.99

Labour

4 persons @ £9.87 per hour for 15 hours £140.05

Overheads		**£**
Rent	per annum	5000
Rates		842
Light		600
Heating		1200
Transport		12500
Total		**15152**

Based on the production of 50,000 units per annum

0.30p per unit times 1000 total 300

Therefore total costs of production are:

£720.04 for 1000 print run or 0.72p per unit.

The cost of distribution, which is carried out by an independent distributor, represents 55% of cover price (£7.99) which is £4.39.

Costs of production @ 0.72 per unit plus £4.39 distribution costs represents a cost of £5.11. This represents a profit so far of £2.88 per unit. Other costs, if they exist are the costs of sales, such as advertising and marketing. However, assuming there are no other costs of sales then the actual cost to the publisher is £5.11 set off against the selling price of £7.99. The differential £2.88 represents profit of around 27% which is a respectable return on capital employed.

The cost of production including distributors costs produces a profit margin of £2.88. This is based on you having established that the market will pay £7.99 for your books. However, there may be situations when you are faced with the need to reduce prices in the face of fresh competition and price cutting. It may be that your competitor has produced a range of books which are similar to yours and is selling them at £5.99. You can go two ways here-maintain your prices and leave it to the consumer to discriminate or re-examine your pricing.

Reducing your product to £5.99 would have the effect of a loss of £2 per item which, when worked back would entail a loss of approximately 90pence per unit. If you were not prepared to tolerate this loss, or were in a position where you could not lose such an amount of money, then hard decisions have to be made.

The overall costings would need to be re-examined to see if any extra savings could be made. For example, many overhead costs are fixed and an increase in overall production could reduce costs correspondingly.

Break even analysis

One technique widely employed in this situation is called break-even analysis. In the example of the book, not enough is lost, even with such a big price production by the competitor, to warrant the need for a break-even analysis. However, there will be situations depending on the nature of a business, where it will be necessary to establish at what point in production you reach a break even level.

As we discussed earlier, expenses can be split into fixed and variable costs. Fixed costs will include all the overheads such as rent and rates and insurance whilst variable costs are those incurred in production itself. The total costs of running the business are therefore the sum of the fixed costs and the variable costs during that period. The more items produced, the higher the total cost but even if nothing is produced fixed costs will be incurred. Therefore, you will need to know the point of production at which you break even.

Calculating the break even point

Whenever you sell a product, part of the proceeds of sale will be used to meet variable costs-the costs of producing a specific item. The rest is applied towards the fixed costs and the remainder, if there is any, will be profit. The remainder, the profit, is referred as the contribution from the sale of the product.

	£
If a product sells for	7.99
And the variable costs are	2.89
The contribution is therefore	5.10

This means that for every unit sold you will receive £5.10 towards the business. If the fixed costs are £450 per week and you have sold 200 units you will have received £1020 contribution from the sales and be in profit. If however, you sell 89 units in that week you will receive £453.90 which will meet fixed costs and leave you in a break even situation. You

126

therefore have established that you need to sell 89 units in order to reach a position where you have broken even. Any less and you will be in a loss making situation, any more and your profit margin will begin to increase. If as a result of reviewing your situation, you decide to reduce prices then you will need to revise your sales forecast

Internal budgeting-budgeting for expected overheads and capital items

So far we have examined the forecasting of the level of sales, the direct costs of the products and how to calculate the gross profit arising from selling products. We need now to look at the other expenses of the business.

Budgeting for overheads

We need to look at the indirect costs associated with business activity, more specifically overheads. Overheads include:

- Rent and rates
- Salaries
- Stationary
- Telephone costs
- Travelling expenses
- Insurance
- Bank charges
- Entertaining
- Depreciation
- Accountancy, audit and legal fees

Rent and rates

If you are leasing a premises then the overheads associated with this are fixed and known, i.e. fixed annual rental, insurance, service charge if appropriate and business rates. If you own the premises outright then the costs will be minus rent. The only unforeseen costs associated with both leased and freehold property will be unexpected repair costs.

Salaries

Wages will include all other associated costs such as employers National Insurance Contributions, pension contributions if any and any other benefits. A global figure for the costs of labour has to be established. These costs can be easily understood throughout the year, as the only variation will be cost of living increases and the occasional increase in NI contributions.

Stationary

This particular item will cover all the costs of stationary throughout the business. It includes company letterheads, envelopes, copier paper and so on. This has to be seen against a backdrop of the previous year's expenditure and can be quite easily ascertained.

Telephone

There are two elements to telephone charges, telephone also including fax:

Rental

Quarterly line rental

Calls

This area also has to be measured against the previous year's expenditure. It is an area that will vary depending on the levels of business. The only constant is the fact that whether business rises or falls the level of telephone activity is likely to remain constant. If you are losing business, calls will be made to potential customers. If your business activity has increased then the phone is likely to be used more. A look at last year's quarterly bills and progress against budget should help you to arrive at a fairly accurate picture.

Travelling

This particular cost will vary widely from one business to another. Certain businesses require very little travel whilst others require extensive rail, air and road travel. Again, this cost will be influenced by the level of business and you should be able to ascertain the broad cost quite accurately.

Insurance

A business will need several different insurances. These include:

- Public liability
- Employers liability
- Building insurance

- Equipment insurance
- Consequential loss insurance
- Product insurance.

Obviously, the nature and type of your business will determine the types of insurance needed. These will be easily identified and the costs fixed.

Bank charges

Banks publish a list of their charges and they should be quantifiable. However, charges can be negotiated so there may be room for improvement in this area.

Entertaining

This particular item will vary depending on the nature and type of the business. Again, you know the needs of your business and the value of entertaining and the costs should be easily quantifiable.

Depreciation

This reflects the loss in the value of capital equipment. This is a revenue expense but has to be discussed further within the context of capital expenditure.

Accountancy and audit fees

The charges from your accountant can be fixed, i.e. one fee is payable or they can vary depending on the charging structure of the accountant used. In addition, the nature and type of service will vary, some companies will use an accountant for all its functions others will use them only for preparation of end of years accounts. Again, you know the extent to which accountants are used within your company and also the likely charges. One other area to consider is that of selling and distribution and the expenses associated with these elements.

These can include:

- Sales representatives salaries
- Commissions
- Travel expenses
- Sales office expenses
- Communications
- Accommodation
- Publicity (advertising)

And any other item associated with this area. You should be in a position, having identified all the relevant cost areas to draw up an administration budget like the one shown overleaf.

Budgeting for capital items

The capital budget is every bit as important as the revenue budget. The revenue budget deals with the day to day running costs and income of the business, the capital budget will deal with the provision of capital items such as machinery, vehicles etc. The capital budget is of more relevance to cash flow than to revenue expenditure and we will be looking at this at little later. Capital expenditure has an impact on profitability in two key ways:

- o By increasing the depreciation charge
- o By increasing the amount of interest payable as a result of borrowed money
- o The timing of capital expenditure can have a dramatic effect on cash flow of a business. It is important to time acquisition of capital items with cash flow into the business as this will decrease reliance on the need to borrow or to spend much needed capital and find your business in trouble.

Example of an administration budget
Period 12 Months to 31st March

	Previous years actual
Current	
Budget	

Materials
Stationary
Other

Salaries and Wages

Management

Clerical

Cleaners

Other

Expenses

Rent and rates

Telephone

Postage

Travelling

Entertaining

Insurance

Bank Charges

Audit and accountancy

Subscriptions

Depreciation

Other

Example of an overall revenue budget
The period 12 months to 31st March

	Products		
	Type A	Type B	Type C

Total

Sales

Cost of sales

_____

Contribution to profit

_____

Selling and distribution overheads

_____

Administration overheads

_____

Budgeted profit

_____

****

Ch. 9

Monitoring Budgets and Cash flows

Effective monitoring of budgets and cash flows entails regular scrutiny, the making of comparisons between what you have forecast and what is actually happening within your company.

On both the budget and cash flow there is a column entitled actual and projected. At the end of each given month it will be necessary to fill the actual column and measure this against expenditure and make appropriate revisions.

If things are seriously wrong then detailed analysis of your business activities is needed.

In many cases, there are crucial timing differences between income and expenditure which can cause problems. A typical budget and cash flow forecast, if all is going well will look like the example below. This is based on a publishing business, which has one month's credit with its suppliers and also gives one-month credit to its distributor. The unit cost is £7.99.

See overleaf for an example monthly cashflow forecast

Monthly cash flow forecast

Sales

Budget	Jan	Feb	Mar	Apr	May
	2000	1500	3000	1750	2000
Sales value	15980	11985	23970	13983	15980
Purchases	7500	5625	11250	6562.5	7500
Overheads	1440	1080	2160	1260	1440
Profit	7040	5280	10560	6160	7040

The planned cash flow forecast should therefore correspond to the one below:

Cash flow	Jan	Feb	Mar	Apr	May
Income					
Sales		15980	11985	23970	13983
Expenditure					
Purchases		7500	5625	11250	6562.5
Overheads	1440	1080	2160	1260	1440
Surplus/					
Deficit	-1440	7040	4200	11460	5980
Opening					
Balance		-1440	5600	9800	21260
Closing	-1440	5600	9800	21260	27240

If, however, your customer is one month late when paying a bill, this will throw your cash flow out and you will have to revise the columns accordingly. Those people who owe you money are called your debtors. Quite simply, they are in debt to you. It is vitally important that you maintain a system to monitor those who are in debt to you. Failure to do this will mean that you will be short of cash and your plan, based on your budget and your cash flow forecast, will not be accurate. It is best, when managing business, to have two sets of records for invoices, one for paid invoices and one for unpaid invoices. Those debtors who are late with payment are called "aged debtors" and the records kept by your self are called the aged debtors records. The analysis you carry out is called the aged debtor's analysis.

It is essential that you have a standard period within which you will send letters to debtors and a cut off period when you will take court action. Even if you pursue the customer for payment in the county court it is never sure that you will recover the debt. However, it is a matter of principle because cash flow management, as we have seen, is integral to your business.

Monitoring budgets

In addition to having to make adjustments to cash flow forecasts because of late payments and other reasons, it may be that you have overestimated your budget figures. In other words, you got the budget wrong. It is obviously very important to check the budget performance each month, i.e. budget against actual to make sure that performance in this area corresponds to your cash flow forecast. Larger businesses will prepare a full set of operating accounts each month in order to ensure that they have an ongoing accurate picture. For small business, this is obviously impractical and therefore an ongoing monitoring of the budget and cash flow forecasts is crucially important. One area which can potentially cause you problems is that of stock. The value of stock will often not vary from month to month though there may be seasonal trends. If the stock does vary a lot, and is giving cause for concern you have two alternative courses of action:

- Take stock each month and evaluate its costs
- Introduce a stock control system. This is the favoured approach as it is less time consuming. You record the amount of each line of stock on a separate account so that you can quickly evaluate its value.

Excessive stocks tie up much needed cash and will be a drain on your company's liquidity. There are a number of ways of deducing the amount of stock that you should carry. The important factors are:

- The amount of sales of that particular product
- Delivery times
- Discount policies on purchase
- The size of raw material batches ordered
- The value of the stock

You should be able to deduce an accurate stock level by looking at previous sales and the amount of stock consumed and projecting this forward to correspond to future sales. You will need a careful analysis of needs because obviously bulk buying at a discount will play a part. However, even if bulk buying, much needed capital could needlessly be tied up. The longer term cash benefits of discount must be weighed against ongoing sales and profit.

The use of financial ratios for monitoring budgets and cash flow

A financial ratio entails deducing the correlation between two figures and ascertaining the meaning of that correlation. There are four types of financial ratios:

- Profit ratios - these show how efficient the business is, or how good it is, at making profit from capital invested.
- Efficiency ratios - these show the management efficiency of the business.
- Liquidity ratios - these ratios measure the working capital within the business
- Solvency ratios-they show how solvent the business is or how near it is to going bankrupt.

Profit ratios

There are three useful ratios, which indicate how profitable your business is:

- The gross profit margin
- The net profit margin
- The return on capital employed within your business

The gross profit margin

The gross profit margin is probably the most important ratio. The gross profit calculates the relationship between the gross profit and sales by the following method:

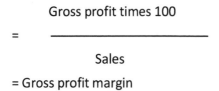

$$= \frac{\text{Gross profit times } 100}{\text{Sales}}$$

= Gross profit margin

The net profit margin

The net profit margin shows you the ratio after the deduction of all expenses of the business except tax. It is not as reliable an indicator as the gross profit margin but can be useful.

It is calculated as follows:

$$\frac{\text{Net profit times } 100}{\text{Sales}}$$

= Net profit margin

The return on capital ratio

The return on capital ratio measures the revenue being generated from the capital employed in the business. This ratio enables you to compare the income produced by the business with income from other forms of investment.

The ratio is calculated as follows:

Profit before charging interest and tax

Total capital employed

= Total capital employed

Efficiency ratios

Efficiency ratios divide into three areas each of which are further subdivided:

- Debtors
- Debtor's turnover ratio
- Debtor's collection period
- Creditors
- Creditors turnover ratio
- Creditors payment period
- Stock
- Stock turnover ratio
- Average stockholding period

The debtor's turnover ratio

These particular measurements show just how efficiently the capital utilised by the business is being used. The debtor turnover ratio shows the number of times that the unpaid debt is "turned over". It is calculated like so:

(overleaf)

Sales (+ VAT)

Debtors

= Debtors turnover ratio

The debtor's collection period

The debtor's collection period is a more useful ratio for measurement. This shows the average number of days that it takes you to collect your debts:

Debtors times 365

Sales + (VAT)

= Debtors collection period (in days)

The creditors turnover ratio

You can check the creditors turnover ratio in a similar way and also the creditors payment period:

Purchases (+VAT)

Creditors

= Creditors turnover ratio

Creditors payment period

Creditors times 365

Purchases (+VAT)

= Creditors payment period

It is important to monitor the creditor period as well as the debtor's periods as you can run into trouble if you yourself become a debtor and run the risk of losing credit.

The final ratios here are the stock ratios. In the same manner as the ratios for debtors and creditors are measured, the stock turnover ratio and the average stock holding period can be calculated in the following way:

The stock turnover ratio

Cost of sales

Stock at cost

= Stock turnover ratio

The average stock holding period

Stock at cost times 365

Cost of sales

=Average stock holding period

Liquidity ratios

Important ratios for any business are those measuring liquidity. The following will be outlined:

- The current ratio
- The quick ratio
- The security interval

The liquidity ratios show the ability of the business to meet its liabilities as they fall due from its assets. A business should have sufficient current assets to cover its current liabilities.

The current ratio

The current ratio measures the ability of a business to achieve this, in this way:

Current assets

_____

Current liabilities

= Current ratio

As discussed, current assets are items such as stock, work in progress, cash in the bank, debtors and cash at hand. Current liabilities are amounts owed by the business to its creditors and bank overdrafts. Current liabilities do not include items such as long term loans, which do not normally fall due for repayment within 12 months.

The current ratio will usually be between 1.5 and 2. If it is less than 1, you are probably relying on a bank overdraft secured on the

144

long-term assets of the business, or delaying payments to your creditors. Whatever the situation, the requirement for working capital should be of some concern. If this ratio exceeds 2 then you may not be making the best use of your current assets. You may have too much cash in the bank or too much stock or to many debtors.

Checking the quick ratio

The current ratio checks all current assets and current liabilities. A better way, or test, is to check on those assets, which are cash, or near cash. This is the relevance of the quick ratio.

Assets such as stock and work in progress may be difficult to sell and covert into cash to pay the liabilities of the business and so these are excluded. Only those quick assets that are left - cash, money at the bank and debtors, are included. The ratio is calculated as follows:

Quick assets

_____

Current liabilities

= Quick ratio

This ratio is usually between 0.7 and 1, although the nature of a particular business will affect this.

The security interval

This particular ratio measures how long the business could survive if no more cash was received but if it continued to pay its normal expenses. It is calculated as follows:

Quick assets

_____

Operating expenses

= Security interval

The security Interval is expressed as a daily figure. This interval is usually between 30 and 90 days, although depends on the type of business.

Solvency ratios

There are two ratios in this group:

- The solvency ratio
- Gearing

If your total liabilities exceed your total assets then your business is technically insolvent. This is expressed as the solvency ratio, expressed as follows:

Total assets of the business

_____

Total liabilities of the business

= Solvency ratio

If this equation produces a ratio of less than 1 then you are insolvent. This is an are that you must keep under careful review, as you may reach a point when you cannot trade due to the inability to meet liabilities. Even if the ratio is greater than 1, you cannot always feel totally secure. This is why the corresponding use of liquidity ratios is so important.

Checking gearing

The ratio of money that a business has loaned to the capital invested in the business by shareholders or the owners of the business is referred to as the gearing of the business. This includes accumulated profits if they have not been withdrawn. It is calculated as follows:

Total borrowed

_____

Owners capital

= Gearing

The gearing of a business is an important guide to how much the business should be allowed to borrow. In general, banks expect their lending to the business to be at least matched by the investment of the owners and shareholders. By using ratios you can check on trends and financial health of your business and also make a comparison with a similar business to your own.

****

Glossary of terms

Accounting ratios-A set of ratios used to indicate a particular financial position of a company.

Aged debtors-This term is used to highlight those people who have been in debt for a longer period than the norm. It is normal practice to age debts in terms of months so that when a debt becomes a problem it requires chasing and settling.

Balance sheet-A statement of the worth of the business at the accounting date expressed in terms of historical cost.

Break even point-The point at which production equals the fixed cost-the point at which you break even.

Budgets-A financial/quantitative statement, prepared prior to an accounting period which forecasts future expenditure. The budget is used as a planning tool and is essential for the effective management of business.

Capital expenditure-Expenditure on fixed assets which have a lasting benefit to the business.

Cash flow forecast-A forecast showing the budgeted receipts and payments for the forthcoming year (or period).

*Credit period-*The period between the supply and invoicing of goods and services and the payment of the invoice.

*Creditors-*The suppliers to the business to whom money is owed and the amount owed by the business to them.

*Current assets-*These are assets which are either cash or can be turned into cash quite quickly. They include cash, bank balances, debtors. Stock and work in progress.

*Current liabilities-*These are amounts owed to suppliers (creditors) together with short term loans such as bank overdrafts,

*Debtors-*Those who owe money to the business

*Depreciation-*An allowance made for the reduction or dimunition of the value of fixed assets.

*Direct costs-*Direct costs are those costs directly related to the production of the product.

*Fixed assets-*Property and equipment owned by a business which will have a long lasting benefit to the business.

*Fixed costs-*A fixed cost is a cost which is unaffected by variations in a firms production. A fixed cost may be rent, rates etc.

*Gross profit-*The profit earned by a business from trading, prior to the deduction of overhead expenses.

*Indirect costs-*Indirect costs are those costs which do not relate directly to the production of the product but are necessary to provide the setting within which the business is run.

*Key ratios-*Key ratios measure the performance of a business in a way that conventional analysis cannot. These ratios are essential to provide a picture of where the business is.

*Long-term liabilities-*Amounts owed by a business which are not due for payment within one year.

*Net assets-*Net assets are the total assets of the business minus its liabilities.

*Net profit-*The profit of a business after taking account of all its expenses.

*Overheads-*Money spent regularly to keep the business running. Overheads include rent, rates, salaries etc.

*Profit and loss account-*An account summarising the income and expenditure of a business for a given period and showing the surplus and deficit.

Quick assets-This is a subdivision of current assets, comprising assets which can realise cash quickly if needed.

Revenue expenditure-Revenue expenditure is wholly used up during the accounting period. Examples of revenue expenditure include raw materials, payment of rent and salaries.

****

Useful addresses and websites

Association of Taxation Technicians

30 Monck Street

London

SW1P 2AP

Phone: +44 (0)20 7340 0551

e-mail: info@att.org.uk

www.att.org.uk

Association of Certified Chartered Accounts (ACCA)

www.accaglobal.com

Institute of Chartered Accountants England and Wales

www.icaew.com

01908 248 250

Institute Members Scotland

PO Box 26198

Dumfermline, KY12 8ZD

0131 1251

Chartered Accountants Ireland

Chartered Accountants House,

47-49 Pearse Street,

Dublin 2

Chartered Accountants House,

32-38 Linenhall Street,

Belfast,

County Antrim

BT2 8BG,

United Kingdom

www. charteredaccountants.i.e

Chartered Institute of Taxation

30 Monck Street

London

SW1P 2AP

Phone: +44 (0)20 7340 0551

www.tax.org.uk

The Association of Accounting Technicians.

140 Aldersgate Street,

London

 EC1A 4HY

www.aat.org.uk

The Financial Conduct Authority

25 The North Colonnade

London

E14 5HS

0800 111 6768

https://www.fca.org.uk/

Government Departments

HMRC

www.gov.uk/government/organisations/hm-revenue-customs

Inheritance tax

www.gov.uk/inheritance-tax

The Insolvency Service

www.gov.uk/government/organisations/insolvency-service

National Insurance

www.gov.uk/national-insurance/overview

Department for Work and Pensions

www.gov.uk/government/organisations/department-for-work-pensions

Pensions-The Pensions Regulator

www.thepensionsregulator.gov.uk

Auto-Enrolment

www.autoenrolment.co.uk

Department for Business Innovation and Skills

www.gov.uk/government/organisations/department-for-business-innovation-skills

154

Index

www.straightforwardco.co.uk

All titles, listed below, in the Straightforward Guides Series can be purchased online, using credit card or other forms of payment by going to www.straightfowardco.co.uk A discount of 25% per title is offered with online purchases.

Law

A Straightforward Guide to:

Consumer Rights

Bankruptcy Insolvency and the Law

Bailiffs and the Law

Employment Law

Private Tenants Rights

Family law

Small Claims in the County Court

Contract law

Intellectual Property and the law

Divorce and the law

Leaseholders Rights

The Process of Conveyancing

Knowing Your Rights and Using the Courts

Producing Your own Will

Housing Rights

The Bailiff the law and You

Probate and The Law

Company law

What to Expect When You Go to Court

Give me Your Money-Guide to Effective Debt Collection

Disabled Children and the law

Mental Health and the Law

General titles

Letting Property for Profit

Buying, Selling and Renting property

Buying a Home in England and France

Bookkeeping and Accounts for Small Business

Tax for Small to Medium Size Businesses

Creative Writing

Freelance Writing

Writing Your own Life Story

Writing performance Poetry

Writing Romantic Fiction

Speech Writing

Teaching Your Child to Read and write

Teaching Your Child to Swim

Raising a Child-The Early Years

Creating a Successful Commercial Website

The Straightforward Business Plan

The Straightforward C.V.

Successful Public Speaking

Handling Bereavement

Individual and Personal Finance

Go to: www.straightforwardco.co.uk